POETRY AS A MEANS OF GRACE

Poetry
as a Means of Grace

BY

CHARLES GROSVENOR OSGOOD

NEW YORK
GORDIAN PRESS, INC.
1965

Originally Published 1941
Reprinted 1965

809.1
Os 2 p
56934
Jan. 1967

Published by Gordian Press, Inc., by
Arrangement with Princeton University Press
Library of Congress Catalog Card No. 65-25106

Printed in U.S.A. by
EDWARDS BROTHERS, INC.
Ann Arbor, Michigan

In memory of

A. EDWARD NEWTON

who loved most the biographical part

of literature—and of life

CONTENTS

POETRY AS A MEANS OF GRACE

YOUR POET

THE FIVE CHAPTERS of this little book found their genesis in a request for advice to young seminarians about their reading.* But their case is not essentially different from the case of all young people who wish to keep themselves articulate and to insure the perennial flow of their springs of spiritual life against the drouth of routine in business or profession.

The first chapter proposes certain general considerations, and offers certain suggestions, one in particular. Each of the other chapters illustrates these proposals with a single literary figure. These exemplars have been chosen for their preeminence, and their fitness to perform the cultural function I have in mind. They are, however, by no means prescribed.

In times like these, if at any time, the religious implication should call for no apology; since I can discover in all criticism no ultimately sound theory which does not with all else take into account the basic human instinct for religion. At any rate I offer these suggestions as the best that I can gather out of such knowledge and experience as I have accumulated through forty years of study and teaching, and more than sixty of close association with the Church. And if in these conferences the clerical audience seems to be assigned to the front sittings, it is earnestly hoped that any who are seated farther away may find themselves within range of the speaker.

In what ways can literature, particularly poetry, serve to refresh and fortify us in the daily and weekly round of professional duties? What, and how, and why shall a minister read

* First designed and delivered as the Levi P. Stone Lectures in Princeton Theological Seminary, 1940.

to keep himself fit for the service of his high calling? Or for that matter, any man who has committed himself to a life of active mind and spirit? This question will be the referee of all that ensues herein.

What, then, shall I read? How shall I economize time and energy, how keep my head above the deluge of books that now overflow the world? Obviously I must learn to swim alone, not be a dead weight on the opinion of others. I must practise to become my own judge and critic.

Now, a critic is not, as some fancy, a mere professional shopping-agent among literary fashions, paid to relieve us of the trouble of making up our minds. In the matter of reading this is a function which cannot be transferred. A critic is one who is in search of permanent values, and who develops a power to recognize them, and the ultimate reasons for believing in them. To train self-reliant readers of this sort is a primary aim of all teaching of literature.

Latter-day critics are likely to judge a work of art—a poem or a picture—statically and intrinsically, by characteristics within the work itself. Is it technically "good" or "unusual"? they ask. Is it conscientious? Is it what the poet set out to make it? What department of life, what tendency, what period, what influence does it exemplify? Is it individual and out of the orbit? What new "approach" does it exhibit?

Experts of the past from Plato to Sidney were more likely to judge a work of art operatively, dynamically, according to its effects upon the listener or beholder. What are the emotions which the work excites? What the action or praxis which springs from those emotions?

Each view is partial, and a reliable and final appreciation must needs include both. To be sure the old way, concerned as it has to be with healthful and unhealthful, safe and unsafe, good and bad, right and wrong, cannot avoid moral issues, though such issues have for some time been out of style, at least in criticism.

It would seem, then, if we are to economize time and energy in our reading, and train ourselves to be our own reliable judges and critics, that we cannot leave out of account the distinction of good from bad, of right from wrong—yes, even of sacred from secular. For on reflection, the greatest single works of art, whether of poetry, painting, music, sculpture, building, at least in the western world, have sprung from religious exaltation, or have been organically involved with it.

This last distinction, between sacred and secular, may at first seem to us obsolete and irrelevant, of concern only to professed ecclesiasts, encrusted with the corrosion of ancient controversy.

It was, however, a matter of agonizing personal concern to men as great as St. Paul, St. Jerome, St. Augustine, and such seculars as Petrarch, Boccaccio, and Milton, with corollary results important to a thoughtful reader in any time.

St. Paul, sophisticated in all the rich pagan culture of his day —well ripened, as it were, in that fat Alexandrian autumn— could not in his regeneration cast out his secular sophistication. It was a part of him ingrained in his very fiber. Must it continue there, atrophied, corrupt, dangerous? "And yet shew I unto you a more excellent way."

St. Augustine agonized over the persistent recollection of his youthful unregenerate passion for the pagan poets, especially for Virgil. Those evil, false tales of passion among gods and men had fascinated him and excited him even to tears; and so they might do yet if he would let them. He was so abandoned to literature in his youth that he had feared a mistake in grammar more than the sin of petty thievery or lying. But "behold, O Lord my King; whatsoever good I have learned, being a boy, unto thy service let it be directed, yea, whatsoever I speak or write, or read, or number, let all serve thee."

But this was sixteen centuries ago, and we are broader of mind today. At least we think we are, in these days of critical irresponsibility.* Some are so "broad" as to say that all literature, all art is sacred. Everything man has been inspired to create is as sacred as Holy Writ itself. If your religion is truly catholic and universal—and the more it includes, the more Christian it is—you will recognize the divine and sacred in every honest work of man. This is an easy, cheerful, generous view.

Others, equally broad and generous, but a bit more mundane, come to much the same result by insisting that all art, all literature, is secular. Even the Bible is but a human document. Present it "to be read as Living Literature," and it really comes true. People discover to their surprise that it is poetic, beautiful, imaginative, romantic, human, like any other secular book of high order. In this light they will read it and buy it and make gifts of it. It might indeed become a best-seller—if it were not already one.

There are still others—few perhaps—who maintain that the Bible, a whole library in itself, contains every kind of book you really need, and, above all, the inspired truth as no other book contains it. Why, then, lose time over secular literature, especially if your calling is the cure of souls? So runs that fabulous yarn about the caliph who burned the Alexandrian library, saying: "If all these books agree with the Koran, they are superfluous; if not, they're lies!" It is a tight argument; yet something reasonable within us rebels against such unlovely, such dangerous aversion to the innocent delight and edifying use of literature.

On the other hand no thoughtful person will content himself with mere sentimental enthusiasms which melt all distinctions in generous warmth of good feeling and tolerance, nor with a mind so broad that it comprehends neither height nor

* See Archibald MacLeish, *The Irresponsibles*.

[6]

depth. But he who intelligently rejoices in his faith will rejoice intelligently in all that God has created, and gain at length an accurate and self-reliant discernment in matters both profane and sacred. You will not need to show him that the Bible is literature, that it is a library of human, wise, beautiful, romantic, and poetic books. To him this is obvious. To him it is transcendent literature and more. And it is transcendent literature just because it is more. It could not otherwise be the Bible, distinguished by its intrinsic spiritual authority from all other books.

Such is the conclusion, final and unalterable, of all who have profoundly and faithfully tested this Book of Books in the laboratory of life itself—among them distinguished savants, men of affairs, soldiers, martyrs, artists and poets, not to mention myriads of obscure and simple but noble men and women whose spiritual authority is just as great.

This host is essentially agreed that the distinction between secular or profane literature and sacred literature is actual and valid and unexceptional; that sacred literature transcends but embraces the secular; that the best that can be derived from the secular is to be won only when it becomes ancillary to the convictions and practice which proceed from an intelligent faith in God, and in the Truth as He has revealed it to us.

I am well aware that such a view is unacceptable to most critics today. Yet years of study and teaching compel me to maintain that by such an ancillary relation, secular literature is not humiliated but exalted, not dimmed but illuminated, not defaced but glorified, not sterilized but fertilized, to the infinite increase and enrichment of the world's language and letters.

Literature serves its best ends, and keeps itself procreative by ministering pleasurably to the spiritual needs in any generation to which it may survive. Instead of leveling sacred literature down to its own plane, profane or secular literature dignifies itself to higher ends, as Virgil is dignified and illuminated by his service to Dante. And as Virgil might not enter Paradise, so secular literature cannot equal Holy Writ in power or authority or efficacy as a means of grace. Yet it may illustrate, reinforce, verify, and illuminate Holy Writ, and warp the world into the range and field of its magnetic influence. It may serve us as the sycamore tree served Zacchaeus, to gain a clearer sight of the Incarnate Truth.

These are well enough as historical or theoretical considerations. But have they anything to do with what, and how, one immersed in the distracting business of a modern office or parish, should read?

Well, what *is* the actual state of things, for example, among the clergy? I have raised this subject as opportunity offered when conversing with ministers of the Gospel, and I can only say what they have told me. Some, they say, do read, here and there; they read books most talked about at the moment, and their professional periodicals, nothing else. Some, they tell me, read nothing. Some think that after doing their best to satisfy the exacting demands of a modern parish they have no time left for reading. Some reason that they have no need of literature; their intimate knowledge of men and women in the most intrinsic part of their lives, all of it generalized and interpreted in the Bible, makes other literature superfluous. Even Shakespeare is unequal to such a combination. The case of the clergy is, in more parlous measure, I fear, the case of the layman.

Others forthwith recognize the obvious, utilitarian value of books. The modern minister must read what is going, what all his parishioners are reading, so that his sermons and conversations—nay, his confessional—may rest on a ground of thought and feeling common with them. Current and popular books offer a certain liaison with the minds and souls of his flock. Granted. Then too he may gather from current books *exempla*, quotations, or anecdotes with which to drive home a point, or reclaim the wandering interest of his listeners at that sagging point, past the middle of his discourse, which every public speaker must look out for. Reading of current books will keep the preacher up to date and abreast with this world which he is trying to serve. He must know what this world of today is thinking, feeling, proposing, and keep just ahead of his flock if he is to lead them. All these books on world politics, on social problems and adjustments, psychology, world economics, science, must be taken into account, even though in two or three years most of them will be obsolete. Very well, take them into account—success in the spiritual life must take everything into account—but learn the shortest cuts, so that this duty to contemporary speculation may be discharged with the utmost economy of energy and time.

How? Well, there are the reviews. And then too the man whose spiritual house is in order, whose mind is made up, can find his way as can no other through the uncharted welter of contemporary literature and books. Use this sense of direction to break your trail through the wilderness of publications, and do not dawdle long and unprofitably over a book merely because the megaphone of a modern advertisement proclaims its primary importance, and this novelty of literary merchandise deploys every specious trick to bait your curiosity. You should as your own critic know the difference between first and fourth rate, and have the courage of your expert knowledge.

I have for years been trying to teach students how to find their way among books. Bacon's trite but useful distinctions between books to be chewed and swallowed and digested, and books to be merely tasted, is relevant. Cultivate the habit of looking first at the table of contents, or the index, or the preface, or all three. Select the cardinal or test chapter or chapters. Find the heart of the book. From that center, read back or forward. Not all of any book is equally important. There are speedier and more reliable ways of knowing a book than beginning at page 1 and reading to page 637, or wherever those heartening words "The End" greet your tired eye. Someone probably says: "But that is so superficial; I'm always afraid of missing something." I still maintain that, when well exercised and practised, it is the most thorough way of reading a book, and the fairest. And this I assert mindful of the reports of intelligent students who in after years have tested it fairly. "No, Sir," retorted Dr. Johnson, "do *you* read a book through?" Yet he it was who always "tore the heart out of a book."

I wonder how much the clergy of today keep in mind the old medieval distinction between the Active and the Contemplative Life. How concerned are they in maintaining the equilibrium between them? When a pastor's soul is weary and confused and short-focussed and out of adjustment from cares and distractions of the parish, he can find readjustment only through the contemplation and influence of things that reach to the infinite and invisible. One of these means is prayer. One of these means is literature. I do not mean just books, but the thing which distinguishes itself from the rest by its imagination, its beauty, its generalization and transcendence over the mere phenomena of life. If any man has within him the depth to which the deep of literature can call—I do not mean that he should be "literary" in the narrow sense—herein is a means of restoration which is efficacious as great music, or pictures, or the grandeur of Nature, or prayer are efficacious to a man whose soul is weary with labor.

I once heard a minister say in effect: "It is the end of the year. I am tired. I keep reading to revive myself, to refresh myself with the best thought of the day, the newest theology and social ethics, but somehow it doesn't work, and my heart and mind are numb and flabby. I need a physical vacation, of course. But much more I need to lose myself—nay, find myself —in the mind of a great poet who has transcended situations, and conditions, and problems of his generation, one who does not date, who is neither new nor old, one who is not merely the voice of his time, but of all times." It was a clear case of what the medieval *dévots* called *siccitas*—spiritual dryness—a malady to which laymen are as susceptible as preachers. He asked me to recommend such a poet, but the choice of course must in the end be his.

Which brings us to a distinction of cardinal importance to our whole reckoning.

For there are three kinds of literature with which we have to deal:

1. Current literature. Much of it is ephemeral, now as in any other age. At any rate current literature has not yet undergone the incorruptible test of time. Think of the books of three or four seasons back which then seemed of such insistent importance. Most of them are gone with the wind. Think of Emerson's advice not to read a book less than a year old. What would you not give to redeem the overtime you gave them. Many of them are by no means negligible, but they have no right to all or most of our contemplative leisure. Beware of literary furores!

2. Books that survive as antiques. These are chiefly purveyed in academic courses in literature as significant documents of how the world has felt or looked or thought in this age or that. The *Works and Days* of Hesiod; the *Thebaid* of Statius; the *Romance of the Rose;* the sonnets of Petrarch; Sir Philip Sidney's *Arcadia;* Sir Thomas Browne's *Religio Medici;* Ben Jonson's *Bartholomew Fair;* Fielding's *Joseph Andrews;* Tennyson's *In Memoriam*—these are but random examples of literary antiques, which nevertheless must contain a considerable element of the immortal, the unfading; else all the professors of literature and all their courses would have availed naught to keep them alive. Yet they date.

3. There is the third kind—the perennial and dateless literature, which rises clear of its times, throws down all barriers of

centuries, and schools, language, nationality, and fashion between its day and place and ours, flashes upon the soul with a
light of truth more intense and convincing than issues from
any book of the first or second class, any book merely of its
own or our day, with the truth as it was in the beginning, is
now, and ever shall be. It is the literature—usually poetry—
which makes us exclaim: "How modern! Why, that might
have been written today. To think that it is a thousand, two
thousand years old!" Its truth is not abstract, aphoristic. It is
never platitudinous. Its truth may lie in its strange power to
snatch a bit of living beauty, either human or natural, grand or
little, with such comprehension and delight therein that it thrills
us with its imperishable reality, its liveliness, its universality,
its just-rightness, its deathless and dateless music; so that however apparently trivial the original fact may have been, the
poet has clothed it with the dignity and grandeur of timelessness. Such instances occur to me as Odysseus cast away on the
shores of Phaeacia; or those two gabbling housewives in Theocritus who took a day off to go into Alexandria from the suburbs
to see the Adonis celebration; or the grief of the Roman
Catullus for his brother; or Alcestis going away with Death in
her husband's place; or one of Chaucer's indelible portraits—
say, his parson; or the wit of Touchstone or Falstaff or Dr.
Johnson; or the flight of Spenser's third hymn; or the elemental
music in Milton or Dante which of its very self confronts us
with the super-reality of things invisible. It is the quality of
those idylls on a Greek urn which so transported the poet Keats,
of Vermeer's View of Delft, for it exists in all the arts. In
literature it manifests itself through such creators as Homer,
Plato, Aeschylus, Sophocles, Euripides, Theocritus, Catullus,
Horace, Virgil, Dante, Spenser, Shakespeare, Molière, Milton,
Pope, Swift, Johnson, Wordsworth. Secular literature of this
sort, *and such only,* I commend to your lifelong contemplation.

For it is such only that can most effectually extend and supplement our experience, can help us to organize that experience in our own minds, generalizing and universalizing it, and bringing all this multifarious world around us into such scope and compass of comprehension, such symmetry of design under divine interpretation, that nothing need surprise us or frighten or jar us out of adjustment, or paralyze our right and timely action in the face of specious counsel. How important, nay indispensable, is such comprehension of life to one who aspires to understand, enter into, and resolve the moral and spiritual perplexities of human beings in all their infinite variety.

But what, in more definite terms, are the effects of such life-long companionship with a great poet? The deepest effects certainly are indefinable. They operate in those abysmal depths of personality which are still a mystery though a tremendous fact. But certain observable and ponderable results there are which follow such perennial association, and which it may be useful to define.

1. Style. I once saw a book which recommended—or seemed to recommend—to the clergy the reading of good literature chiefly for its effect upon their style. The theory is excellent, but capable of shallow construction. The author seemed to say: "Read Macaulay enough and you will come to speak like him." Heaven forfend! Macaulay wrote an excellent style. So did Dr. Johnson—and Johnson wrote sermons for his clerical friends. But you would not do well to go stalking about in formal Johnsonese, like the Reverend Josiah Crawley of Hoggle End in Trollope's *Last Chronicles of Barset*. I am probably unfair to the adviser aforesaid. He may have meant simply that a good deal of Macaulay, or any congenial artist equally skilful, will be a wholesome tonic to your style, especially if you get certain of his ringing passages by heart. We have the undeniable examples of Augustine and Jerome and Dante and

Milton, and for that matter all good men who accepted the discipline of Grammar and Rhetoric, which in the medieval Trivium meant Literature, who justified their study of pagan and secular authors as the means of polishing and reinforcing their style to the glory of God.

They knew well enough that style was not a matter of mere imitation, of formulating into rules the rhetorical practice of a great master, or of writing according to those rules. Style is partly that, of course, and I for one think that we have latterly too much neglected these methods of cultivating good style. But its sources are deeper. Literature is strangely procreant. Vigor and grace beget vigor and grace. Wit begets wit. Said Falstaff: "I am not only witty in myself, but the cause that wit is in others." Style is a matter of reinforced personality, of intrinsic powers, of a reliable sense of values; and the power and quality of a man's utterance, whether colloquial or formal, is determined and tempered in the deep ranges of his nature, not alone on the level of mere skill and technique. A man in daily contact with say Johnson or Dante, or whoever his chosen seer may be, with their vigor, their wit, their imagery, their deep sense of the world's tragedy, their struggle to turn it to account in terms of beauty or truth or behavior, will inevitably catch from them something of their sense, their feeling, their intellectual and spiritual thrust, which is bound to assert itself in the quality of his own expression and his ministrations. It cannot be otherwise. In this deeper and subtler way the style of your speech grows stronger and purer under the influence of a great poet, while it becomes more distinctly and peculiarly your own.

2. Secular literature rightly understood does not contradict, nor try to contradict, sacred literature. Rather, within its secular range, it validates spiritual values, illustrating and verifying them from a wide census of human experience.

Sacred teaching provides us with a vast poetic frame of all-inclusive compass. It is our business to fill this frame with the substance of our living. But we are human and fallible and little, and our conception of the frame's compass tends ever to grow narrow and inadequate, leaving outside much that should be included, failing to take into account spacious areas of life and many various specimens and kinds of human nature and experience. Our own limited contact with the world may not be enough. In secular literature we shall find much material with which to fill out this universal frame, thereby gaining on the one hand a more adequate sense of its inclusiveness, on the other a more expert and reliable sense of values among things secular.

Let me illustrate our commonly inadequate sense of this frame's vast dimensions. Sometimes we discover a man of learning or high eminence and consequence who is also of the Faith. We are a bit surprised and elated—shame upon us— and get excited over a believing scientist or scholar or author or statesman. Why should we? Is not our conception of the Faith large enough to include such? Of course the man believes if he is great enough to contemplate all-inclusive truth—if, as Johnson says, he has ever thought about it.

Some people are unhappy for fear the frame of the Faith is not strong or large enough to withstand the strain of the World. They point out instances, especially among young people going to college, of spiritual disaster from such over-strain. But it is just such narrowly inadequate faith that cannot stand the stress of adjustment to include a larger world, a faith weak because it has not exercised itself in the broad air and expanse of life itself. And literature provides that air and expanse, lending fullness and substance to one's faith, authenticating and expanding it to include all comprehensible things within its compass. Thus literature helps us to draw human life into right relation to the Eternal Verities in our own minds, the only relation in which it can take on complete meaning or design.

3. It follows that literature may be a means of spiritual sophistication. This may be but another way of saying what we have just said. Somehow the world seems to labor under the notion that preachers, and teachers too, are an unsophisticated class. Taking sophistication in its deeper sense, the world is wrong. Perhaps the most unsophisticated persons to be found are among businessmen in a large city. Be that as it may, let us distinguish between spiritual sophistication and what I may call spiritual provincialism. I have known clergymen and teachers—so have you—who, troubled by the world's charge that they are unsophisticated, have tried to meet it by erasing the marks of their profession and showing themselves regular fellows. How much more provincial this than a steady reliance upon the dignity of their profession and function. It is not necessary for them to step out of their profession to prove their sophistication. If a man's sympathies and understanding are broad enough, whether he be cleric, teacher, lawyer, business-man, he will have no mark of any particular profession— which, Johnson says, is the essence of good breeding.

There is such a thing as a spiritually minded man of the world. Such indeed have been the most unworldly and illustrious Christians. How gloriously manifest in them is their spiritual sophistication. Nothing and no one can surprise or overawe them or catch them unawares. Observe St. Paul or St. Augustine or St. Francis or Sir Thomas More, or Bunyan or Wesley or Phillips Brooks or any other great Christian as they move about among men. They are always self-possessed, unembarrassed, because they have taken into account all things that matter. To many of them literature has been a means to such spiritual sophistication, extending their knowledge of the world beyond the reach of their actual experience, bringing a larger and larger accumulation of material within the scope of their appraisal. To most of us it may serve the same end, that we too may not be taken with embarrassed surprise by anything with which we have to cope. It lends us vicarious experience, and the world in its clumsy way will recognize and respect the self-possession and authority, not to say the consequent good manners and gracious behavior and urbanity that go inevitably with spiritual sophistication.

But someone may object that I claim for literature what one may find in much fuller measure in life itself. People say that life even in a small town will teach you all about human behavior that you can learn or need to know.

I love a small town. So, I find, do most Americans who have ever really known one. Up to early manhood I was bred in what was then a small and isolated country town. I owe that blessed town an immeasurable debt for what it taught me about Nature and Man, yes, and Literature. It endowed me with a heritage which has proved to be of priceless value and incessant use in my subsequent life, professional and otherwise. But such knowledge and experience alone is not enough. Literature is necessary to expand this limited field of vision. It breaks the bounds and enlarges the petty compass of existence. It presents human life in magnified instances, emphasized, generalized, clothed in idealized form which lends them the irresistible and convincing beauty of art. And to turn back from such instances to the small specimens of real life presented by our daily routine, is to understand actual life as we could not otherwise understand it, to see it rightly appraised, dignified, clarified; as Shakespeare, for example, takes a sordid tale of *mésalliance* and slander and raises it to the *n*th power in *Othello*. In the light of that vision of mischief how much more wisely and truly can we observe, measure, and perhaps relieve the mischief of scandal in that neighborhood around the corner. In the light of the career of Milton's Satan or Eve, how much more easily can we recognize and deal with silly social pretence, or over-reaching greed, or ambition, or the mortal dangers of selfishness and wilful boredom. In the light of Dante's love for Bea-

trice, how immeasurable appear the consequences for infinite
good of the deepening intimacy between those two promising
young people in your parish. Literature helps us to see as important what is really important, though the world call it a
trifle, and to see trifles as trifles, though the world call them
important; like Lazarus in Browning's *Epistle of Karshish*,
who returned from death to live on, newly aware of

The spiritual life around the earthly life.

Thus literature, especially great poetry, extends the range
of vision, intellectual, moral, spiritual; it expands the compass
of our sympathy; it sharpens our discernment; it corrects our
appraisal of all things. Such powers we recognize in all the
great priests of sacred history. And if we could consult them,
I fancy most of them would bear witness that no secular agency
had been more efficacious than literature in giving them that
authoritative ease among men and ideas, that spiritual and
social sophistication which characterizes them all.

4. Literature, especially poetry, is probably our most powerful agent for rousing, sensitizing, and energizing our sense of
beauty in all things. This practical modern world is prone to
conceive beauty as an extraneous luxury—adornment *appliqué*
—and in religion, as perhaps a danger. We do not think of it
as an integral and inseparable element of our living, as did the
Greeks; or as did the Christians for many centuries. Yet something deep and instinctive within us hungers for the beauty
of holiness, as well as for its truth and its righteousness. Plato's
identification of the Good, the True, and the Beautiful was no
mere formula. Beauty is an indispensable and logical part of
practice and worship in the religious life. Yet is this generally
evident in our churches, our services, our hymns and music,
our offices and sermons, even in our manners and behavior as
churchmen? Many excellent people are, I think, repelled by the
unloveliness of our religion, which not only arrests in them an

instinct to worship, but makes them feel that in such conditions the beauty of the Lord is not to be apprehended. We sometimes think they are fussy, and say that if they are so troubled by what is external, their religion cannot go very deep. But the essential beauty of religion is not external—it goes very deep. All through its history the Faith has instinctively tried to express this inner beauty outwardly in its churches and in its worship, and has slowly built both of them toward a perfection beyond the attainments of mere secular arts practised by secular artists. Its architecture, painting, sculpture, music, poetry are proof enough. Beauty is an intrinsic element of the Faith, whether it is manifest in a person, a service, a ministration, a tone of voice, a building, or a dooryard.

> Who sweeps a room as for Thy laws
> Makes that and the action fine.

The protest of Protestantism was necessary, but it cost us a price in this respect. It has now and then endeavored in vain to repress the irrepressible human instinct for beauty, with the result that the instinct has expressed itself abnormally in pretentious, raw, unlovely forms. The Church has sometimes shown itself aware of its uncomeliness and tried to mend it. The Oxford Movement of Newman and Keble was a case in point.

The beauty of religion must be an outward manifestation of beauty within. It cannot be a mere cosmetic gratuitously applied, nor does it consist in mere external embellishments, such as bad Gothic and factitious, ephemeral rites and symbolism. The craving for Beauty, whether alive or dormant, is deep and normal within us all. It is an essential element in our sense of the Divine. To be safe and reliable the sense of Beauty must be commensurate with the depth and height of our spiritual life, that is, with our sense of Truth and Righteousness. It cannot then be satisfied with the bleak dreariness that too often manifests itself in our Church and its ministrations.

Sense of Beauty is more than ordinary "good taste." At its best, indeed, good taste follows inevitably from a true sense of Beauty. Nor is a sense of Beauty mere historical knowledge of the arts; nor is it a fancy for what is pretty, or taking, or grandiose. It includes a sense of form, structure, proportion, of the beginning, middle, and end of an organism of art, and of their logical and functional relation to each other. It includes a sense of what is fitting or appropriate in time or place or relation. It includes a sense of more than meets the eye or ear. It includes a sense of that super-reality and timelessness that lies behind genuine manifestations of beauty, however transient that manifestation may be. It includes a sense of the ultimate valuation of all these things in terms of human life, and of the intimacy which they bespeak between the human and the Divine.

But the sense of Beauty is no more a matter of wholly unconscious growth than other forms of regeneration. Sometimes it finds its proper nourishment in Nature—mountains or sea or stars or change of seasons; or in the arts of men—architecture, painting, music. But I think that no other secular agent so well serves the needs of the greatest number as great literature, particularly great poetry. For great poetry embodies and illustrates and fulfills all requirements of order, proportion, and the appropriate and fitting—what the old critics used to call decorum. Its medium is language, the same as the medium of the preacher's or teacher's art. It deals, like the other arts, with Nature and human life, just as profoundly as they, and more explicitly. It is directly concerned with cause and effect, with act and consequence, with passions high and low, with the beautiful and ugly possibilities in human relations. Furthermore it exercises that strange power which it shares with the other arts, a power of intimating truth irreducible to mere words, a power more convincing than argument, more direct than statement, more compelling than proof. Such qualities of great poetry, asserting their quiet influence upon us for years, cannot fail of their outward effect upon our bearing and ministrations, rendering them more fit, more orderly, more luminous.

Lest such reasoning may seem too theoretical, let me explain that in following it I have been guided by actual cases which I have known—men whose ministrations to the spiritual needs of men have been most substantial, deep, and durable. They were men constantly and actively susceptible to the beauty of holiness as manifest in great poetry.

Perhaps someone is saying to himself: "But I have no literary sense." Or, "I never had any good courses in literature." Or, "I never had any at all." Or, "All this talk about poetry and art and such doesn't make sense. It sounds like an esoteric jargon of highbrows altogether removed from this world of reality." Beware lest you rationalize what you imagine to be your own defects. It is a subtle temptation.

Literary sense is closer to common sense than many people suppose. It does not demand a natural talent for words, a ready agility with pen or tongue, a knack for technical criticism. I have known instances in which these very talents were an actual hindrance to the genuine appreciation of poetry. For a genuine sense of literature I would insist rather upon a man's passionate interest in the human individual, on his passionate concern in the spiritual life of men, in the issue between failure and success, between perdition and salvation. Such is the indispensable basis of a full, true, and responsive sense of values in literature; for literature is life, with the same scale of values, the same ineluctable laws, the same unerring and beautiful justice.

Since no one will have sufficient time for all the greatest poets, I suggest the preferential choice of one. He need not exclude the rest, but one should have right of way over the rest to your attention and study.

And this is a choice that you must make for yourself.

Whatever else you read, adopt one of the greatest poets as your own for life, one with whom habitual companionship and deepening acquaintance become a more and more abundant source of refreshment and strength, a confirmation of spiritual truth, an elevation to a more comprehensive view of life.

Choose this author as friends are chosen, less by deliberate selection than by natural congruence, such as that which leads to the growth of the closest friendships. Let this author be one who is in your case congenial and responsive. Think of him daily in odd moments. Read a bit of him as often as you can, until at least parts of him become part of yourself. Do not consult other books or people by way of explaining him any more than you can help. Know *him* first of all. Let him explain himself. What you thus come to know in him will every day seem new and fresh; every recourse to him brings forth new thought, new feeling, new application, new aspects of things familiar. He becomes an antiseptic against all the agencies that tend to make life sour, stale, and insipid.

And this is the one practical suggestion that I have to make. But in making it I bear in mind what Virgil became to Augustine and Dante and Milton; what Cicero became to Jerome; what Plato and Platonism became to St. Paul and Spenser; and what, in more obscure but perhaps more relevant instances of my personal acquaintance a single poet or literary genius has effected in the intellectual and spiritual growth and sustenance of the individual.

I propose in the four remaining chapters, to exemplify this suggestion by four preeminent literary figures—Dante, Spenser, Milton, and Johnson. I have chosen these examples partly from long acquaintance, partly because they lend themselves with peculiar aptness to the purpose we have in mind. I should have been glad to choose only English poets, but Dante's claim is too strong.

Someone is saying: "Why not Shakespeare?" Why not indeed? He is most interesting and is never dull. He charms us with his humor and thrills us with his truth to life. He is memorable in his wit, most illuminating in his observations of human nature, most impressive and true in his setting forth of moral cause and effect, of action and reaction in individual and collective cases, a creator of noble and even adorable women and men, a pure and spontaneous singer.

> His poet's eye, in a fine frenzy rolling,
> Doth glance from heaven to earth, from earth to heaven;
> And, as imagination bodies forth
> The form of things unknown, the poet's pen
> Turns them to shapes, and gives to airy nothing
> A local habitation and a name.

Compared with the others he is an incomparable recorder of phenomena. As Arnold says:

> Others abide our question, Thou art free.
> We ask and ask: Thou smilest and art still . . .
>
> All pains the immortal spirit must endure,
> All weakness that impairs, all griefs that bow,
> Find their sole voice in that victorious brow.

Arnold may have meant this as unqualified praise, but he is saying in effect that Shakespeare is not conclusive about what he has so well observed. He is never prepared to say that his mind is made up. We can only guess at his conclusions, if he drew any.

Choose Shakespeare by all means if he is your man. He will give you recreation, stimulate you, impart to your style of utterance the necessary vitamins and graces; he will sophisticate you, enliven and refine your sense of beauty, open your eyes to much that you would never see without his help. But I should not expect of him much help in polarizing the phenomena of life into the harmony of one living and active conviction.

Arnold may after all be rationalizing his own inability to make up his mind. He voices the fashion, in these tentative days of relativity, of supposing that a really great mind proves its greatness by not making itself up, or at any rate by not revealing its conclusions. Only a small mind will be hardy enough to jump to a conclusion; a great mind knows better. And if all the other great poets differed radically from one another in their conclusions, if each made up his own mind in a different direction, if their conclusion of the whole matter were in each case a mere guess, and a different guess, there would be little to choose. But such is not the fact. For in essentials, as far as their respective civilizations admit, they converge. And this agreement, this conclusion in secular or profane poetry, has often been a comfort and assurance to me, a confirmation of faith through which the whole phenomenal world has been drawn within the scope of that faith.

Choose therefore your own poet. You alone can recognize him. Learn his language, be it Greek, Latin, Italian, German, French—or English. This is easier than it sounds. But stick to your man, *approfondissez*, as the French say. Slowly sound his depths, year in and year out; explore your Hell and Purgatory in life—and there will be plenty of both—with him at your shoulder as Dante had Virgil at his. Only thus can you deploy and economize the vast resources which await you in secular literature. Again like Virgil, it may bring you to the summit where the ascent with Beatrice begins.

DANTE

IN THE FOREGOING CHAPTER I proposed as the first principle of an economy in reading, the choice and adoption of one great author. This author, presumably a poet, should by nature be congenial, born to become your lifelong companion and monitor, day in and day out the most intimate member of your intellectual household.

I have known men and women—perhaps you have also—who are incarnate proofs of this principle, who have educated themselves by ever deepening intimacy with a great literary genius and his work. The exemplars of such educating genius here set forth I have selected partly for reasons aforesaid, but also because I could name for each one of them a man or woman I have known who, perchance missing the academic process, has amply made up for it through the perennial influence of one or other of these as his or her chosen associate.

Some other poet may fit your particular case better, but that is of small moment, since the use and method is essentially the same in any case. Only I should urge that the poet of your choice be great in certain particulars which I shall here enumerate.

1. The poet you choose should be focal. That is, he should gather up into himself in highly intensified power as many as possible of the cultural influences which precede him in civilization. Thus Dante holds in intense focus the great civilizations preceding him: Hebrew tradition, fused with Plato and Aristotle and Virgil and Statius, from which he derived by the distilling power of his genius the essence of classical tradition as no mere scholar could derive it; to this Dante adds, out of

Provençal poetry, the medieval refining of romantic love, its song, its courtly manners at its best, and its idealization of womanhood; to this, the long tradition of Christian ritual, liturgy, and symbolism, which had been enriched and glorified by centuries of ministration to countless sick and needy human hearts; and to this the ripening fruition of human observation and thought in science and theory; but above all he possessed the ordered conclusion of thirteen centuries of Christian meditation and experience as embodied in many writings, particularly in the vast *Summa Theologiae* of Thomas Aquinas, who died when Dante was nine years old. With this complex inheritance he enjoyed the expert technique in reasoning, the skill in the ordering of thought and ideas, which was imparted to those who really entered into it by the ancient scholastic training of the Trivium and Quadrivium, particularly its discipline in Logic. Thus Dante was the high focus of the best which a score of preceding centuries had achieved.

2. Your poet should be a man of encyclopedic stature. Those men were encyclopedic who included within their scope, if not within their actual knowledge, all things which the mind can contemplate, men who took into account all things which can be an object of human knowledge, in the heaven above, the earth beneath, or the waters under the earth. Furthermore in Dante's day men did not, like us, view this knowledge as divided into exclusive departments, subjects, specialties, but as various aspects of one thing. Politics, science, literature, the arts—liberal arts, fine arts, or applied arts—philosophy, religion, were to them inextricably interwoven and blended; and in Dante's case at least all were subject to Theology in the grandest sense. The advantage of such a view while it lasted, and could last, was of immeasurable value to the poet, and determined the completely rounded order and reliable conclusions of his work. Yes, it even dictated the otherwise incomparable music of his song, its perfect modulation and harmony. Con-

trast with this the present dissipation of our knowledge, our crying need of such encyclopedic minds.

But the focal mirror in which they of old beheld the whole compass of creation was of small and convenient dimensions compared with ours. Since then it has been expanded and strained under the stress of more recent theory and discovery until it has burst into a thousand fragments, and our views of the world today are perforce fragmentary, incomplete, partial. As a result our observations are timid and tentative. Our very language betrays our uncertainty. We are always talking about our "approach," our "attitude," our "viewpoint"—flimsy terms—instead of our conviction, our conclusion, our belief. *Credo* is an unfashionable word.

How far off the new synthesis is awaiting us no man can say. Until the time of its advent how imperative is our need of knowing men who in other days achieved the encyclopedic view of life, when no doubt it was easier to achieve. Yet I am convinced that when the new synthesis shall have been achieved, and shall have effected its permeation of human life, it will again be, in essentials, the same as that of Dante, or Spenser, or Milton, or Johnson, or Plato, or St. Paul, or any other of the great encyclopedic minds. It will be, must be, a religious synthesis.

3. The poet you choose should be inexhaustible. You remember Johnson's familiar retort to Goldsmith's remark that the Club needed new members because the present ones had pretty much travelled over each other's minds. Said Johnson: "Sir, you have not travelled over my mind, I promise you!" Choose one whose mind you can never wholly explore. Such is each of these exemplars. Ever since Dante's day this exploration of his mind has been going on.

At Cornell is the greatest collection of Dante in the world. Its huge catalogues list some 8,375 titles, a number much increased in the twenty years since the catalogue was last revised. I daresay the profoundest student of Dante would be the first to declare that he had never travelled over the vast expanse of that mind. A veteran teacher of Dante in one of our universities tells me that he reads the *Divine Comedy* in Italian three times a year, and never without discovering new values, new ideas, new beauty. I speak of these dimensions, not to dishearten but to encourage a prospective reader of Dante, to indicate the measures of those intellectual spaces in which he can enjoy free and happy range, where he will ever discover something new, new not because it supersedes the old, but because it confirms and enlarges it. It is like the increasing intensification of light which Dante experienced as he ascended through the ten spheres of Heaven, to gaze at long last upon the Celestial Rose of the saints exalted, and the Light Eternal

> that in thyself alone
> Abidest, alone thyself dost understand,
> And lovest and smilest, self-knowing and self-known!*

> O luce eterna, che sola in te sidi,
> Sola t'intendi, e da te intelletta
> Ed intendente te, ami ed arridi!

And yet in that very Light of Lights Dante recognizes his own human image, like Browning's Lazarus returned from the other world.

> O heart I made, a heart beats here!
> Face My hands fashioned, see it in Myself!

In selecting Dante as an exemplar, instead of an English poet, it occurred to me that certain young people love and enjoy the expansion of mind and ideas which comes with the adventure into a foreign tongue. Strictly, no translation of a poet is possible. There are men who keep up their Greek, and daily have their few minutes with Homer, or Euripides, or Sophocles, or converse in their own incomparable tongue with Virgil or

* All English quotations of Dante are from Jefferson B. Fletcher's translation, used here by permission of the translator and the Macmillan Company.

Horace. Adopt any one of these for the elder brother of your soul, and you will have my wholehearted blessing. If you are drawn to him as man to man, his language will be no obstacle. The old bugbears of grammar and gerund-grinding and drill will turn to kind and pleasant playmates.

Begin with a good English translation of the *Divine Comedy*, noting the passages which appeal to you most on first reading, and leaving the more difficult ones for later consideration. Get a few lessons in Italian. Read your favorite passages, if possible, in an edition which prints the English on one page, and the Italian opposite. Such explanation as you need you will find in Toynbee's *Dante Dictionary,* the smaller edition. In Italian the commentaries of Scartazzini or Fraticelli will be enough. This is a small outfit, but should suffice. Stick to the text, first, last, continuously. Commentators are your servants, and one or two good trustworthy ones, ready to come when needed, are better than a milling crowd who block your progress and cut off all access to the man you most wish to see and know.

4. Your great poet-elect will be a man of deep, passionate, and reasoned humanism—one who not only can observe the varieties and values of human experience, and is in deep and understanding sympathy with human beings as such, but who cares what becomes of them, deplores their manifold follies, adores their more beautiful or heroic manifestations, and so far as he can penetrate the mysteries which beset us all, may become their guide and advocate in adjusting their lives to the Eternal Verities, in short, laying hold upon their salvation. Such is Dante.

5. Your great poet will also be a singer. What with our print and silent reading we are rapidly growing stone-deaf to that most beautiful of all music, the music of poetry. We *must* hear again, if we will see and learn—not for the pleasant titillation of the ear, or the physical delight of infectious rhythm, but because it is through the subtle sounds of poetry that subtle and

difficult meanings are conveyed more powerfully than by any argument devisable in the mind of man. All great poets are singers in a very sober sense. Until the ear is attuned to their song, we cannot comprehend them, nor what they have to say. They all agree that music, harmony, song, are basic, and when they draw nearest unto that which is elemental, their voices grow most musical. Meter is not a mere adventitious ornament of language, which we can measure and classify. Dante's glorious *terza rima*, as it is called, may be described as a succession of five-stressed triplets rhyming a-b-a, b-c-b, c-d-c, etc.; but as you keep hearing it, it becomes ever more charged with meanings not conveyable in prose, a gleaming chain, slowly dropping, glittering link by link, from that invisible world into which Dante's imagination penetrated to the full stretch of human ken, down to the level of our mundane apprehension.

6. The great poet will also show his greatness by his power to breed poetry in others; and in Dante's case this power has never waned, from Petrarch in the generation after Dante to the present; not only has he enabled countless little poets to add a cubit or two to their stature, but his great brothers in song—Chaucer, Milton, Shelley, Byron, Browning—have welcomed his help and thriven upon it.

7. Poets of this prolific power have always recognized the right partnership between the craftsmanship of poetry and inspiration. They insist upon learning the trade as a trade that can be learned. Dante talks about this a great deal. He wrote three treatises, the *Vita Nuova*, the *De Vulgari Eloquio,* and the *Convivio,* dealing at least in part with this matter. There are plain sober rules to be mastered and practised in the making of a good poem—rules for manufacture, like a carpenter's rules for the management of tools and the various woods he works in: the manipulation of words, of figures of sound and speech and thought, of meters, of design and forms of construction. Lesser artists either ignore these, and trust only to the

excitement of creation which they take for inspiration, or else go to the opposite extreme and think the technique of poetry is the whole of it.

But Dante, while he gave just and high value to technique, believed with his whole heart in inspiration, in that strange dissolution of his own mind in something greater—those unforeseen and incalculable periods when vision and idea and power of expression coincide as it were under some mysterious outside control; and after the period is over, behold the new work of art born into the world—how, not even the artist himself can tell. If you are a man of genius, prepare yourself by hard work in acquiring conscious skill for such moments, and when they strike you will prove the fit and efficient medium through which the unseen will create the evidence of itself in a new and great work of art. Such capability of inspiration, such moments of self-oblivion, are the evidence and proof of genius. Dante knew them, and thereby knew his own greatness. In the Limbo at the entrance to Hell, Dante at Virgil's side met an extraordinary quartet consisting of Homer, *poeta sovrano* (poet unsurpassed), Horace, Ovid, and Lucan, who all did honor to Virgil. After a word apart with Virgil they turned and saluted Dante himself and

> paid me yet the greater deference
> Of making me one of their company;
> And I was sixth among such sapience.

This is not unbecoming vanity, but a decent consciousness of his own powers. Yet his confidence in them was not such that he could count upon them at any moment, and he pauses repeatedly in his poem to appeal for the inspiration outside of himself. Such invocations of Muses and Apollo are more than conventional gestures. The desperate heart of the great artist is in them.

The poet of our choice, then, should be focal and encyclopedic, inexhaustible, a true humanist, a singer, a breeder of poetry in others, and a thorough master of his craft.

Dante was born a Florentine in 1265 and died in exile at fifty-six, in 1321. In that brief time he occupied a point of vantage, a height of civilization which looked every way; far in both directions—back and forward. It was a point of high but unstable equilibrium. Italian medievalism, chivalry and the romantic cult of love, the scholastic philosophy and its technique, the encyclopedic conception of knowledge, the fine arts of painting through Giotto and Cimabue, music through Dante's friend Casella, a new sense of classical antiquity whose ruins were on every hand, the cult of poetry through the poets of Provence, the discovery of new poetic possibilities in the Italian tongue, the grand summary and interpretation of centuries of thought by Aquinas—it was a coincidence of ripeness which demanded the synthesis of a great poet, and which placed him in a position of peculiar advantage. Of all of these cultural elements Dante made himself master. Taken in its lowest terms, viewed in its most superficial aspect, his *Divine Comedy* is a museum of medieval curiosities. But it is more. Dante evidently had the prehensile eye of great genius:

> Mine eyes which were intent to see and know
> Things that in novelty might give delight.*

His very similes reveal an eye which overlooked nothing. Among the host of people he passes in his journey through Hell, Purgatory, and Heaven are not only many he has known, but others he has heard of, in or just before his own time; historical figures from any past time; mythological figures; Biblical figures; one as real as another, whether or not their fame has survived.

* *Purg.* 10.103-4.

On his ascent through Paradise, in the fourth circle, the Heaven of Mars, where abide the soldiers of the Faith, Dante meets the soul of his great great grandfather, a stalwart old Florentine, Cacciaguida, who had lived and fought more than a century and a half before Dante, and who had perished on the Second Crusade. This doughty ancestor of the poet discourses at length on his own conspicuous career, on the simplicities of the good old days in Florence, on various of the first families—enough to show, without display or vanity, that Dante himself was of aristocratic and proud social position in Florence.

The imaginary date of Dante's vision is 1300, but of the actual writing various times soon thereafter. In the one hundred and fifty years from Cacciaguida to Dante, Florence had changed. With all its glorious luster, its breeding, its arts, its intellect, its beauty, Dante's town had a dark reverse side. Florence was a paradox of good and evil, great and small, worst and best. It had grown rapidly rich, splendid, materialistic, sceptical, corrupt. It had become hopelessly involved in the political squabbles of the two parties, Guelf and Ghibelline. Whatever the original issue in this quarrel, it had by Dante's time well-nigh disappeared. A hard and dreary business it is to follow the course of these violent and deadly quarrels as they raged throughout north Italy, between city and city, family and family, clique and clique. If one can discern any issue at all it was that the Ghibellines fought for strong imperial influence from outside to keep order, and prevent these Italian cities from bleeding themselves and each other to death. The Guelfs, on the other hand, fought that the Italians might be allowed to manage or mismanage their own affairs. There was indeed no Italy such as we know. The unit was the city manipulated by the tyrant family which had usurped power in each. In Florence there was as yet no such family. The Medici had not arrived. But amid the new architectural splendors and gorgeous life of that old free city raged a hot and deadly conflict, as family quarrels are usually the worst. Two Guelf factions, the Whites and the Blacks, were swaying back and forth in a life-and-death struggle so desperate that no one could tell what it was all about, except that certain families, Dante's included, were aligned on this side or that. Dante's family belonged to the Whites, who to help their cause, finally allied themselves with the Ghibellines outside of Florence, though the two factions were originally both Guelf. Dante had taken a conspicuous part in public affairs. When he was thirty-six, the Blacks got the upper hand, and Dante, on false charges of graft, was banished, with all the rest of his party, and was sentenced to be burned alive if captured.

He left behind him a wife and four children, his property, and associations with places and people which were inexpressibly dear to him; and for the rest of his life, nearly twenty years, he wandered in lonely exile. His stout old ancestor Cacciaguida foretold it:

> Thou shalt prove how salt to taste is e'er
> Another's bread, and how the path is hard
> Which goeth down and up another's stair.
> And what will bow thy shoulders most of all
> Will be the bad and foolish company
> With which into this vale thou needs must fall;
> For all, ingrate, insensate, and malign,
> Will turn against thee. . . .*

At length he will find himself a lonely party of one—like every true idealist.

Thus he wandered from city to city, court to court, through Italy even to Paris, and possibly to England. At one point his sons, now grown up, joined him in exile; and when he was past fifty an amnesty gave him permission to return, but on terms so humiliating that Dante rejected them with scorn.

* *Par.* 17.58-69.

Bitterly homesick, hoping day by day that his great poem might yet win him an honorable homecoming, looking wistfully beyond the Alps, and longing for the advent of the great emperor who would restore order in Florence and drive out the wolves, dreaming at night that he was happily back "in that fairest sheepfold where I slept a lamb," he dragged out the weary years.

But beneath the turbulent surface of Dante's life ran a strong and even current that bore him on to the fulfilment of that destiny which was given him to minister to the whole world through the ages. He seems to have been aware of it. Near the end of the *Paradise* where Beatrice's radiance has at last transcended the power of his song, Dante says:

> Ever since I beheld her that first day
> Still in this life, until this sight of her,
> My song hath gone, unchallenged, on its way.

> Dal primo giorno ch'io vidi il suo viso
> In questa vita, infino a questa vista,
> Non m'è il seguire al mio canto preciso.

At the tender age of nine he had first set eyes upon Beatrice Portinari, then a child of eight. With an unconscious instinct he seems to have recognized in her the necessary complement to himself. Call it love, even in these children. Stranger things have happened. His tongue was loosed, something released in him the power of song. And as this power strengthened through the years, so strengthened and mounted the power of love within him. Beatrice married one of the banking Bardi family at twenty-one, and was dead at twenty-four. Dante himself married a few years later. Somewhere, somehow, in the ten years between her death in 1290 and 1300, the alleged date of the vision of the *Divine Comedy,* when Dante sees Beatrice again in the Earthly Paradise, he forgot the safeguard of her love, fell from grace, and lived in a way which fills him, now again in her presence, with bitter and tearful shame.

> He turned his footsteps into way not true,
> Pursuing the false images of good,
> That bring no promise to fulfilment due.*

Now in the desolation of his exile the power of that old love returned to him, regenerating him, transcending its earthly bounds to become a light which lightened not only the darkest recesses of his life, but shone into the regions of things invisible, beyond the jealousy of his neighbors, as Cacciaguida tells him,

> Beyond the punishment of their perfidy.

Out of such supreme suffering and ecstatic joy, such depths and such heights, such hell, such purgatory, and such heaven, was born his great *Divine Comedy*. He tells us that the making of it caused him to waste away, and again and again he reveals in it his agony of composition, his despair of sharing with us his pain and his ecstasy. He is enjoined by various spirits whom he meets, particularly by Beatrice, to tell all men of what he has seen.

> If a timid friend of truth I show
> Myself, I fear lest I live not for those
> Who will account this time the long ago.†

It is thus clear that he intended his poem to reach even us, in the twentieth century, and ages beyond.

Such then is Dante, a luminous figure standing unmoved against a black background,

> Four-square against the blows of chance—‡

proud, uncompromising, stirred to deep rage against injustice, greed, treachery, and selfishness; interested in everything, with

---

* *Purg.* 31.129-132. † *Par.* 17.118-120.
‡ *Par.* 17.24.

superhuman capacity for love and tenderness, too great for one age, dateless, universal.

Out of the iniquity of his generation he rises as one of the remnant "that shall again take root downward and bear fruit upward"; one of the few to redeem the evil day in which he lived. Which must inevitably be a comfort to us in days like these.

For a moment let us pause to review the symmetrical structure of Dante's Universe and the corresponding structure of his poem. There are the three parts—Hell, Purgatory, Heaven. The poem numbers 100 cantos—the traditional perfect number. Otherwise all proceeds by 3's, 7's, and 9's, numbers traditionally sacred. With one preliminary canto, there remain 99 symmetrically distributed—33 for Hell, 33 for Purgatory, 33 for Paradise. Each of the three divisions even ends with the same word—*stelle,* stars. Dante accepted the old Ptolemaic cosmology, enriched and poetized by centuries of human belief and song. He had no choice. In the center this earth, a stationary globe, with Jerusalem on top, or at the North Pole, the mountain of Purgatory at the bottom or South Pole, and Hell inside. Around the fixed Earth, radiate and expand the nine concentric spheres of Heaven or Paradise, bearing, in order, from center outwards, the Moon, Mercury, Venus, the Sun, Mars, Jupiter, Saturn, the Fixed Stars; then the Primum Mobile, and last and outermost the empyrean or region of the Celestial Rose and the Presence of God Himself in the central Sea of Light. Within the Earth, Hell descends conically in nine concentric narrowing circles to the center of gravity. Hell is thus divided: Ante-Hell, to canto 3; Upper Hell through Circles I to V, cantos 4 to 7; Lower Hell through Circles VI to IX, cantos 8 to 34. Of these last, Circle VII is further subdivided in three subcircles—*cerchetti*—of the Violent; Circle VIII into the ten horrible *Malebolge* or Evil Wallets, confining the Fraudulent;

and Circle IX into four frozen compartments for four kinds of Traitors. Everything is definite and clear and of convenient compass, until we begin the dizzy ascent into the infinite reaches of Paradise, where Time and Place melt away.

Nothing could be more definite in intention. The year is 1300, the season Easter. Dante spends Good Friday and Holy Saturday descending through Hell. At the bottom and center of gravity he and Virgil find themselves suddenly reversed, and they climb upward to emerge at the foot of the Mountain of Purgatory at the South Pole, which they reach on Easter morning. Easter is spent on definite schedule in Ante-Purgatory; Easter Monday and Tuesday they climb through the seven circles that wind about the mountain, and half of Wednesday passes in the Earthly Paradise on top of the mountain. Amid the eternities of Paradise time is not marked. But before that Dante gives even the dimensions—the Ninth *Bolgia* is 22 miles around, the Tenth is 11 miles around.

All this definition, this clear exactness of specifications, is more than a matter of literary carpentry. It is the outward manifestation of the dialectic order in Dante's mind and education. Dante knew its uses in giving form and power and enduring strength to the great work he was appointed to create. And this love of order is most salutary for any of us who have to compose and communicate our thoughts, especially in sermons, speeches, and lectures. Let us ask ourselves: "Have I the sense of form and logical structure, the power to present my convictions in right order? Can I reason?" This habit of order is the indispensable basis of expression. Without it other gifts— personality, plenitude, humor, imagination, wit—are dissipated and squandered. Nor does this order come about by mere following of rules and prescription. It must be rather an instinct, an insistent habit of mind, superinduced or cultivated as it was in Dante's case, by association with minds of like sort. I cannot conceive of a man in daily association with Dante whose mind would not come to practise and insist upon the right ordering of his thoughts and the methodical, progressive expression of them.

Yet to Dante his love of Dialectics, of orderly reasoning, of scholasticism, was not all. These were useful only as maidservants of higher realities—the teaching of Holy Writ, Love as the metaphysical basis of all reality and all values.

> Let not of too great confidence be born
>> Your judgments, lest ye shall become as those
>> Who count, before 'tis ripe, the standing corn,
> For I have seen amid the wintry snows
>> The briar show itself all stiff and wild,
>> And bear thereafter on its top the rose.*

The briar of dialectic is indispensable to the rose of poetry.

Somewhat the same distinction underlies the difference between Dante's Virgil and Beatrice as allegorical figures in the poem. The earthly wisdom of Virgil may be a sufficient guide for a man through Hell and Purgatory, through the mysteries of wrongdoing and retribution, as practical matters, but it requires the Heavenly Wisdom of Beatrice to illuminate these primal matters in their essential values, in their relation to the Absolute, the Eternal, the Infinite. Virgil is the enlightenment of profane literature and wisdom, Beatrice is the illumination of the Holy Spirit through Holy Writ and the power of Love.

All the powers and virtues of the greatest poets Dante embodies in almost even and equal proportion. But none grows more impressive, the longer one's acquaintance with him, than his variety. On his long and exhausting journey through Hell, Purgatory, and Heaven, Virgil and Beatrice hurry Dante, and Dante hurries us, from one strange experience to another, until it seems as if his invention were inexhaustible. Like Dante we would often linger, fascinated by the beauty or personal interest or provocative suggestion of this episode or that; and indeed

* *Par.* 13.130-5.

that is just what we are able to do in a lifetime of familiarity with this poem and this poet. Mere externals, like the Gothic grotesqueries of the imp Malacoda and his antic crew prodding the grafters, in the Fifth *Bolgia,* are as interesting and memorable as is the vigorous shindy of the carvings at Vezelay or Wells, or such as lurk under many a choir-seat in cathedral or parish church anywhere in England. And there are repulsive horrors—boiling pitch, the rain of hot sand and fire, suffocating tombs, the ice encasement of the traitors in the lowest circle —matter too strong for our more tender humanitarian senses, yet having its moral and allegorical values in the final effect of the poem upon us.

We may sometimes disagree with Dante's judgment in detail. There are those poor unbaptized infants condemned "without hope to live on in desire." In the same eternal hopelessness is Virgil whom Dante so adored; for all that it was his Fourth Eclogue, sometimes called the Messianic eclogue, which converted the Roman Statius and saved him. Yet Virgil must for ever abide in Hell. But our disagreements are petty and are bound to be merged into the transcendent rightness and justice of Dante's compelling, even overwhelming, conviction as a whole. For his conviction, based upon his experience with life both sweet and bitter, with men both very good and very bad, upon hard-headed methodical reason, illuminated by a love which came to transcend all earthly love, was the most reliable conviction to which a man can attain. What sympathetic reader of Dante can resist Dante's suasion to lay hold upon this conviction for his own?

The poem abounds in rare moments to which the reader returns again and again. The lovely episode of the helpless Paolo and the child Francesca caught unawares in the storm of a guilty passion, which caused Dante to swoon for pity, has often been exhibited. Ugolino, in the Traitors' Hell, has been made famous by Byron; and Ulysses in the Eighth *Bolgia* of

Evil Counsellors inspired Tennyson's greatest poem. The meeting with the musician Casella in Purgatory was transmuted by Milton in a sonnet. But there are countless other memorable moments—the terrible glowing towers of the city of Dis; that thrilling moment at the end of the *Inferno,* after the long, weary review of human sin and retribution, when Dante emerged and "saw the beauteous burdens of the sky. Thence came we forth to see again the stars." There are great nocturnes:

> It was the hour which makes the heart to swell
> Of those at sea, and homeward turns desire,
> The day that they have bid sweet friends farewell,
> And which the pilgrim, newly on his way,
> Pierceth with love, if from afar he hear
> Bells that do seem to mourn the dying day.

There is that slow dawn across the sea from the beach of the Ante-Purgatory:

> Color of orient sapphire, sweet and clear,
> Now gathering upon the quietness
> Of all the air unto the farthest sphere,
> Opened anew unto mine eyes delight.

Venus and the Southern Cross are still visible. The morning breeze takes flight before the victorious dawn, and from afar Dante sees, as Greek and Roman poets long before had seen, and many another since, "il tremolar della marina." The dew is heavy, the sky deepens to orange, and with the rising sun, from the far horizon, the Angel of God moves swiftly toward us in a crescendo of light.

The reader may find incidental delight in the living portraits, chiefly of Dante's contemporaries and friends, which punctuate the poem. There is fat, good-natured, gluttonous old Ciacco wallowing in the mud of the third circle, to the very life. There is the lazy Belacqua, the maker of musical instruments, and perhaps like Dante a good amateur, contentedly loafing a lifetime away just outside Purgatory, so indolent that he had put off repentance and spiritual adjustment of his life to the last moment, even now drawling out a lazy hope that somebody may pray for him to shorten his time of waiting. But you suspect it cannot make much difference to him; he never did like to hurry.

But nothing is more memorable or more moving than the moment in the Earthly Paradise near the end of the *Purgatory*, when Dante recognizes his lost Beatrice descending from the symbolic chariot and turns instinctively to Virgil:

> Soon as upon my vision smote the high
> > Virtue, which had already pierced me through
> > Before the age of boyhood had passed by,
> I turned me to the left as trustingly
> > As to its mother runs a little child
> > When it is frightened or in misery,
> To say to Virgil: "Scarce to me is left
> > A drop of blood that trembles not: I know
> > The tokens of the ancient flame." But reft
> Had Virgil left us of himself—even he,
> > Virgil, sweet father, Virgil, unto whom
> > For my salvation I surrendered me.

Beatrice speaks:

> "Dante, albeit Virgil disappears,
> > Weep thou not yet, weep thou not yet; for sooth
> > Another sword must give thee cause for tears."

The sound of his name on her lips drew his eyes to hers. And she with stern dignity:

> "Look at me well; I am indeed, indeed,
> > Beatrice. Thou, how deigned'st thou seek the Mount?
> > That man is happy here didst thou not heed?"

Meaning, ironically, "How could you leave your wayward and abandoned life to come to a place of felicity like this?"

Dante is stung with the reproof, his eyes fall in shame to the stream that separates them, but seeing there his own face reflected he looks down to the grass at his feet. Suddenly he hears the angel voices singing: "O Lord, in thee have I trusted; let me never be confounded."

> As snow among the living rafters massed
> Along the back of Italy congeals,
> Drifted and packed by chill Slavonian blast,
> And then, if breathe the land which shadow lacks,
> Melting, it trickles away within itself,

so the music melts his agonized soul into a hot flood of tears. Then Beatrice tells how after her death he had forgotten her and

> turned his footsteps into way not true,
> Pursuing the false images of good,
> That bring no promise to fulfilment due.

Not even the dreams which she had sent him availed to recall him, so low had he sunk, until Beatrice herself, at the hest of the Virgin Mary, descended into Hell and commanded Virgil to conduct him through the vision of Hell and Purgatory, through penitence and purgation, to his salvation. At this point, and in this episode, all the elaborate allegory, the complex imagery, the multitudinous details of the *Divine Comedy* seem suddenly to clear, and its validity to every man capable of spiritual dissatisfaction and longing becomes apparent. Love, beginning even on its lowest terms in the human heart, is a regenerating force, powerful beyond all others, to draw a man out of his animalism, to develop and direct his energies wisely and aright, to enlighten him with a reliable sense of true values, to bear his imagination aloft until it can lay firm hold on the truth beyond the reach of mere reason, even into the presence of God Himself.

An allegory of Hell, Purgatory, and Heaven, by a mystical, medieval poet! Small likelihood that it could contain for us any reality, any authentication in life and the world as it is.

Which makes the solid reality of Dante's poem the more astonishing. How has he achieved it? From time to time a hardheaded, homespun proverb brings us to earth. His hundreds of similes Dante derives from his closest observation of the most ordinary facts. I see his otherwise unoccupied but questing eye fixed like a painter's upon a casual operation or detail such as no one else would notice. In most exalted or unusual moments he summons a simile from the humblest and most usual levels of life. Peasants, cooks, tailors, soldiers, children, blind men, wayfarers, gamblers, criminals, laborers in a Venetian shipyard suddenly appear with the vigorous reality of a painting by Goya or Velasquez or De Hoogh. Sheep, ants, cranes, jackdaws, and common objects of common use and occurrence such as wax, a crossbow, a mirror and candle, a clock, a glass of water, bells, melting snow, clearing weather, serve his realistic purpose. Agnel, a grafting thief of Florence in the Seventh *Bolgia,* is slowly turning to a serpent.

> Just so along before the kindling play
>> Of flame on paper runs a dusky streak,
>> Not black as yet, and the white dies away.

Or,

> Ripples of water in round vessels glide
>> From centre unto rim, from rim to centre,
>> As these are tapped within or from outside.

So thrills Dante as he recognizes how the words of St. Thomas and Beatrice agree. On one occasion Virgil's frown succeeded by kindness begets a simile which develops into a homely and realistic idyll:

> What time in the still youthful year the sun
>> Tempers his looks beneath Aquarius,
>> And somewhat of the night has southward run,
> When often on the ground the hoar-frost casts
>> A counterfeit of his white sister's face,
>> Though little while his pencil's temper lasts,

The peasant, running low in his supplies,
   Gets up, and looks, and sees the countryside
   All whitened over; and so slaps his thighs,
Goes in again, strides up and down, and mopes
   Like a poor soul who knows not what to do;
   Goes out once more, and gathers then new hopes,
Seeing the world to have an altered face
   That little while; and now takes up his crook,
   And leads his sheep forth to their grazing-place.

We have already observed the memorable reality of Dante's portraits. Many of them—most of them—are of people who, whatever their importance in their day, have been forgotten. Some of them cannot now be identified even by the most patient research. Toynbee's *Dictionary*, a *Who's Who in Dante*, is indispensable, and a beginner sometimes finds his patience tried by these many personal interruptions. But he will discover that no one of these persons mentioned by Dante is just a person, obscure or forgotten; no one of them has escaped that universalizing power of the great poet to lift the particular out of the particular into grander proportions and significance; so that even the least of the folk set in the immortality of his poem has been endowed by him with the life which makes his case true, not only in the twelfth or the thirteenth century, but in the twentieth or any other. His people have a way of sometimes turning into our contemporaries, of assuming modern guise and identity.

Of course the ultimate reason and basis of this enduring and burning reality in Dante's poem is the intensity of his own living, his high ecstasy and vision, his fierce participation in the turbulent affairs of his time, his love of Florence, his disappointment in her and in himself, his shame, his misery, his exile, and, transforming all, the purification of his boyhood passion for a little girl. Some would argue that Beatrice is merely an imaginary ideal, that the Dante of the *Divine Comedy* is a wholly rationalized Dante, not identical with the poet in his habit as he lived. I cannot see it. Nor do I see how any man who has shrunk with horror from the depths which underlie every life, who has found an escape from such hell through his love for others, through their love for him, a love which interprets the Love that transcends human limits, can blink or deny the reality of Dante's poem as embodying actual concrete events and feelings of his life.

This reality is seated deeply in Dante's moral conclusions, his convictions about sin. He inherited of course the medieval classification of the primary and deadly sins as seven—Pride, Envy, Wrath, Sloth, Avarice, Gluttony, and Lust. It is a grand list. For completeness it will stand any test of real life. It has been built on centuries of laboratory experience in the cure of souls. All the subtler sins of selfishness, which is Pride, of deceit and dishonesty and despondency, proceed from one or other of these seven, or are identical with one or other of them, in its largest sense. Of these seven the spawn is legion.

But Dante, in his Hell at least, curiously shifts the emphasis. He disposes of four: Lust, Gluttony, Avarice, Sloth, which last he faintly mentions, in the first four of the nine circles of Hell, the first seven out of thirty-three cantos. We then enter the Lower Hell, which begins with the dreadful City of Dis and its angry mob. It deals with the sin of Wrath or Violence. The next nine cantos or so are devoted to the punishment of those who have habitually done violence either to their neighbors, to themselves, or to God. Then follow the fourteen cantos of the terrible *Malebolge,* ten of them, in Circle VIII, devoted to the punishment of the Fraudulent: panderers, seducers, flatterers, simonists, soothsayers; grafters, including a monk who was the Big Boss of a graft-ring; hypocrites; burglars and thieves; evil counsellors; scandalmongers and schismatics; and in the lowest *Bolgia,* plain liars, impersonators, alchemists or fakes, counterfeiters, and false accusers. It is a pretty inclusive list of the sins of dishonesty and insincerity and uncharitableness—those sins we hate most because they come closest to us through politics and public life, through trade and business, nay, through our intercourse with each other, in the daily texture of our lives. And Dante hated them, in Church and State, even more than we, because they permeated like mortal disease the fabric of his society everywhere, and set him adrift in body and soul for all those bitter years. In the Third *Bolgia* are two popes, Nicholas III and Boniface VIII; and thither will pass Clement V, the pope still living as Dante wrote; and frozen among the traitors is Archbishop Ruggieri of Pisa. Dante had courage.

It is these dozen or more cantos, of all those in the *Inferno*, that we can read with especial understanding and sympathy and terror, yet with a salutary satisfaction; for here is a man who can express for us as we would express it but cannot, our helpless abomination of all dishonesty, all insincerity, everywhere, even in ourselves.

But there is dishonor deeper than any of this, and even more hateful, and that is the dishonor of treachery. Encased in ice, in the lowest circle of Hell, bowed, weeping frozen tears, endlessly fighting and biting each other, are the traitors—traitors to Kin, to Country, to Guests, to Friends; among these last, Lucifer and Judas.

Why did Dante devote three-fourths of the *Inferno* to such sins as these, yet hardly mention them in the *Purgatory* except by implication, or in digressive indictment of his times? Why, unless he believed that they are the subtlest, most deadly, least curable, most destructive sins of all? As we look abroad upon the world in its present evil case, can we fail to see his belief confirmed? But from a world so corrupt and abandoned as his Dante did not turn helpless away, and seek escape in his art or in selfish preoccupation with his own salvation. The philosophy of escape of which we hear a good deal nowadays would not have attracted him. It would have savored too much of the deadly sin of Accidia or Sloth. Terrible as is his repeated indictment of conditions and persons of responsibility in his times, it is never a cry of despair. God is not indifferent. He will repay. There is a remnant of good men and women in the world, enough to save it. Above all, the darkest places in his own life and in this world of perverse men he now saw revealed in their true values by that light which had first dawned for him in his boyhood love for the child Beatrice, which had indeed grown dim after her death, but which in his later life and affliction again brightened, grew intense, and expanded, reaching downward, upward, and afar, until Visible and Invisible, Here and Hereafter, became unmistakably clear before him.

For Dante was a mystic—one of those rare persons who has found it possible by self-discipline, contemplation, longing, to pass the barriers of sense and attain to the very presence and sight of God. This consummation he actually achieves in the last canto of the *Paradise*. The matter-of-fact world is usually suspicious of mystics as men of disordered mind. But Dante's mysticism is sane and reasoned beyond ordinary sanity. It was by Love that he had achieved the vision. Love to him is never sentimental or passing. It is the ultimate metaphysical basis of reality, the essence and element of all our living. Love is the inclination of the will toward that which seems good. Love may be perverted to bad objects; it may err in excess or deficiency; it may be selfish, leading to envy, competition, revenge, greed. All things, mortal and immortal, are but a projection of the Perfect Love, that is God, into the contingencies which make up the world. These contingencies when not perverted yearn naturally back to the Perfection whence they came. That yearning is Love. Love thus is a reciprocal attraction, mutual between Infinite and Finite. To us its most compelling manifestation is the Supreme Sacrifice for our redemption. As a sense of that love dawns in us by grace, and by the light of our best love for

each other, so it increases in us, drawing us upward into a
clearer vision of God. Such love it was, he says, which

> Hath drawn me from the sea of love perverse,
> And of true love hath set me on the shore.

> Tratto m'hanno del mar dell' amor tôrto,
> E del diritto m' han posto alla riva.*

When Beatrice has cleared one of his doubts as they ascend in
Heaven, Dante exclaims

> O love of the first Lover, O divine,
>   ... who so bathest with thy words,
> And warmest me, that quickened life is mine,
> Mine own affection reacheth not such height
>   As would avail to render grace for grace:
>   May that All-seeing One who can, requite!
> I see now how is never satisfied
>   Our intellect till there illumine it
>   That truth beyond which is no truth beside.
> In that it rests, as wild beast in its den,
>   So soon as it attains it; and attain
>   It can: vain else were all desires of men.†

It thus appears that Dante's mysticism, and his repeated in-
sistence that Love is the only source of life, are based, not upon
sentiment, but upon hard-headed reasoning assisted by Plato
and Aristotle; that they are authenticated and tested by bitter
and disillusioning experience, but in their final proof fulfilled
and consummated by a realization of God's love expressed
through the life, sacrifice, and triumph of his Son.

What then may we expect from long and continued association with Dante? First, he will bring us into close intimacy
with the rich tradition of Christian worship and experience, its
inheritance of beauty and symbolism, its noble and fitting use

* *Par.* 26.62-3.   † *Par.* 4.118-129.

of the arts, music, painting, poetry, to the glory of God. Transmitted through his sublime poetry these traditions live as they could not possibly live in histories. And I can conceive that they may thus through pastoral ministration subtly transfuse the texture of our present-day worship, making it more significant, appropriate, profounder, more beautiful and helpful.

Then, constant association with Dante must necessarily affect the quality of your style of expression, not by superficial imitation, but by the subtler and deeper influences, giving you order, clarity, beauty and even music of utterance, enriching your fund of illustration and instance, opening your eyes to varieties in human life which you would not otherwise observe, and thus fortifying the authority with which you speak. Indeed, Dante has preachers of the Gospel well in mind, for in the twenty-ninth canto of the *Paradise* he finds room for a most edifying comment on preaching in his day, or, for that matter, at any time. He shows clearly what makes preachers go stale, he points out some of the warning symptoms, and does not fail to prescribe the only remedy and safeguard. If I were preaching, I should wish to have this passage constantly in mind.

We have asked ourselves how many of the clergy, or indeed of us all, guard our equilibrium between the Contemplative and the Active Life. It is preoccupation with the Active Life which, I suspect, is responsible in our day for so many lapses among young clergymen from spiritual ministration, their first business, into mere "social" studies, work, and activity. I would not belittle the importance of such work. Indeed I think it is too important to be cut off from the tap-root of all its life and permanent effectiveness, namely religion. Dante found the true balance between the Contemplative and the Active Life. He can help us to preserve it. He may serve us as Virgil served him, answering our questions as we go our way observing man's iniquity, his efforts to purge himself, his struggle upward to the vision of the Truth which alone will make him free.

An old friend of mine, his life long a teacher and scholar, one whose influence has enlightened a host of young men and women, has through all the years kept up his association with Dante. Not long ago he said: "Dante, beyond all other poets, throws all things into true spiritual perspective." How indispensable that perspective is to any of us who would qualify in service to those who are floundering in confusion, in distorting fears, in paralyzing regrets or self-distrust, in bitter preoccupation with their own troubles.

Men have, I suppose, always been too much concerned in things visible. Especially is this true of the last three centuries or more, with the rise of the scientific habit of mind. I applaud the achievements of Science, and thank God for them. But its habitual concern with things visible and material is partial. It awaits and demands correction by equal concern for things invisible, which constitute the greater reality. "Credo in unum Deum . . . Factorem . . . Visibilium omnium et Invisibilium." So says the old Creed. Nor can we handle or interpret the Visible aright, if we submit to the distortion of this or any other age. As an English wit has remarked: "An unbelieving age is one without invisible means of support." It is a new awareness of things Invisible, the spiritual realities, for which the age is dying, and by which it must die if its vision is not restored. Dante asserts and makes us feel constantly the immediate presence and transcendent importance of the Things Invisible.

In the last canto St. Bernard prays to the Virgin that Dante may finally behold God. This prayer, one of the most exalted things in all poetry, concludes:

> And I, who ne'er for my own seeing burned
> More than I do for his, now proffer thee
> My every prayer, and pray it be not spurned,

That the last cloud of his mortality
    Thou scatter with thy prayers, so that to him
    May be revealed supreme felicity.
Also I pray thee, Queen who canst fulfil
    Whate'er thou wilt, all his affections sound,
    After so great a vision, keep thou still;
And cool his human fevers with thy care.

And then the vision at which even Dante's great power of song fails.

Such as he is who seeth in a dream,
    And the dream goeth, and the mood impressed
    Bideth, nor more may memory redeem,
Even such am I; for almost faileth me
    The vision, yet the sweetness born of it
    Distilleth in my heart perpetually.

O grace abounding, whence I daring won
    To fix my gaze upon the Eternal Light
    So long that I consumed my sight thereon!
I saw within its depths how it receives,
    By love together in one volume bound,
    What through the universe is scattered leaves:
Substance and accident in interplay,
    Fused as it were together in such wise
    That this whereof I speak is one clear ray.

Within the triple Circle of Infinite Light the poet discerned, as it seemed, our own human image.

Trace
I would how to the circle was conformed
    The image, and how there it found a place;
But wings had not been mine for the high aim,
    Save that my mind was smitten suddenly
    As by a lightning-flash—and its will came.
Here power failed to the high fantasy;
    But now, as turns a wheel all evenly,
    My will and wish began to turn with Love,
That Love which moves the sun and every star.

⎍⎍⎍⎍⎍⎍⎍⎍

SPENSER

⎍⎍⎍⎍⎍⎍⎍⎍

I HAVE CHOSEN Edmund Spenser as an exemplar not only for reasons already given, but because I have known him now these many years, and been in almost daily converse with him. I think I know too the kind of man to whom he belongs as a spiritual companion, and who belongs to him. There, for example, is John Wesley. In prescribing a course of from three to five years of liberal education for young women, he included under Poetry, *Paradise Lost,* parts of Shakespeare, Tasso, Young, and headed the list with Spenser's *Faery Queen.*

What might John Wesley find in Spenser? John Wesley, who read Homer on horseback, and was always in such a hurry that Dr. Johnson complained: "Wesley's conversation is good, but he is never at leisure. He is always obliged to go at a certain hour. This is very disagreeable to a man who loves to fold his legs and have out his talk, as I do." Busier than most of us think we are, Wesley found time, and reason too, for reading Spenser. Such a man could tell us something about the uses of Spenser in particular, and secular literature in general. Would that he could take over at this point.

Spenser was not only one great preacher's poet, but is distinguished by the honorary title "the poet's poet," conferred by Leigh Hunt or somebody a century ago, and likely, for good reasons, to stick. Milton found him "a better teacher than Scotus or Aquinas," that is, better than the great scholastics who taught Dante; yet not a teacher by mere precept or doctrine. His influence has been steady and continuous since his time, not much subject to vagaries of fashion in taste or criticism. He is less at home perhaps in our world of today than at any time heretofore, and yet I can think of no poet, except possibly Dante, of whom the world has more need.

Spenser qualifies as a "sovran" poet for lifelong association by the seven tests which we have enumerated.

1. He is focal. Coming nearly 300 years after Dante, he finds himself born into the high excitement of the English Reformation and the Renaissance of Elizabeth. The medieval framework of doctrine so necessary to Dante's great poem was weakening, swaying, and in places crumbling. Yet much of its accessory beauty of idea, symbolism, ritual, architecture, and art was still a deeply intimate part of everyday English life and naturally available to Spenser, who made glorious use of it in his poetry.

But England was for the first time coming to realize her own greatness as England, with the excitement and intoxication and dreams of the future that pulse and flame through the art of Marlowe and Shakespeare and Spenser himself, and give Elizabethan poetry and music that peculiar spontaneous fullness, sweetness, warmth, and light which English poetry has never been able to recapture. Spenser stands where he can look backward and forward to advantage, and brings to focus in his poetry the best of what he saw and foresaw.

2. He is encyclopedic. His actual library was probably not so large as ambitious source-hunters have made out. But one who got the best for his purpose out of Plato and Aristotle; out of the Greek and Roman poets, especially Homer, Hesiod, Theocritus, the Hymns, Virgil, Ovid, Horace; out of Petrarch, Boccaccio, Ariosto, and Tasso; out of Ronsard and du Bellay and Marot; out of the welter of medieval literature and story still available; out of innumerable minor poets; out of all the history, English or general, he could get, even though in the course of his busy and ill-provided life he had sometimes to resort to second-hand means—such a poet adequately measures up to encyclopedic stature.

3. He is inexhaustible. For this I can only offer my word. Turn to him when I will and for whatever reason, the old familiar cadence, image, idea, have a way of seeming as fresh and dateless as bright morning sunshine or the deep breath one draws in midocean.

4. He is human. It is customary to compare him unhappily with his more famous contemporary, and to conclude that his men and women do not live. To the casual observer, I grant, they have not the obvious life of Shakespeare's, nor their variety. There are, however, Britomart and Satyrane and Una, and a dozen others. Humanism is not measured by variety of personalities. With long association one finds that the life of the Elizabethan world which leaped and throbbed in Spenser's veins has permeated the substance of his work and the personalities and deeds and souls of his people, and lent essential human reality to his supposedly faery world. He is indeed human.

5. Spenser is, of English poets, preeminently the singer. For the century and a half since Chaucer the English language had been disintegrating, it seems, losing resonance and timbre and pitch, like an old instrument long since forgotten in the attic. It had become, thought competent critics, no longer capable of poetry and song. In this dark hour, to wit in 1579, when he was about twenty-seven and Elizabeth had been Queen for twenty-one years, it was Spenser, in his anonymous *Shepherds' Calendar,* who restrung the old instrument and called forth the first new enchanting strains. These he was in a few short years to bring to a fullness and range which have helped to keep English poets singing ever since.

6. For no English poet has bred so much poetry as Spenser. From Milton down to minor and even minim poets, they all confess by word or by performance that, whatever they had to start with, they became, every singer of them, more the poet for Spenser. I catch them time and again tuning up their

melody, priming their imaginations, warming and regulating and clarifying their moral and philosophical ideas and enthusiasms by Spenser. The Spenserian stanza, the greatest single metrical invention in English poetry, was but a part of his vast service in this kind.

7. But Spenser was not, any more than any other great poet, just a singer warbling his native woodnotes wild, bursting into artless song just because he could not help it. That is a pleasant but not practical notion that some have of how poetry is composed. Like Dante, he had learned his trade. He became expert in the use of his tools. Spenser was thoroughly schooled, chiefly under that marvellous old teacher Mulcaster at Merchant Taylors School in London, in the grammar, rhetoric, metrics, and design of the Roman poets. He never lost this training; indeed the technique which he gained by it became so ingrained and habitual that however high his inspiration, however powerful the afflatus, this technique was constantly operative, directing, articulating, economizing, and enhancing the glory of his song.

He qualifies, then, by our seven canons. He is focal, encyclopedic, inexhaustible, a humanist, a singer, a breeder of song, an artist.

In all these respects and more Spenser had much in common with Dante. They were both idealists, poets plunged into a world of affairs for which they had a certain relish but to which they never succumbed. Both of them resorted—had to resort—to an outside world of their own invention in order to say their say: Dante to Hell, Purgatory, and Heaven, Spenser to his world of Faery. It was not a deviation to escape reality, but to gain the free scope necessary to their genius. Both of them employed allegory as the most natural, the most practical poetic means of transmission between the ideal and absolute world as they apprehended it and this mundane life of ordinary fact. Both of them toughened the temper of their song in homesick exile. Both believed, heart and soul, in Love as the basis of all reality, the propelling force and medium, the living principle, in all spiritual ascent and achievement and vision.

But Dante, for all his gentleness and compassion, impresses us with a certain imperious and rigid authority. The power of Spenser is rather a subtle suasion slowly insinuating and increasing until it possesses and controls us by a kind of spiritual incantation, or rather a spell, of moral suasion. He was aware of this, I think, and is pretty explicit about it.

"It is most true," he writes, "that such poets as in their writings do labor to better the manners of men, and through the sweet bait of their numbers, to steal into the young spirits a desire of honor and virtue, are worthy to be had in great respect."

Years before he had proclaimed it the poet's glory

> to restrain
> The lust of lawless youth with good advice,
> Or prick them forth with pleasance of thy vein,
> Whereto thou list their trained wills entice!

Spenser, unlike Dante, was of humble, cockney origin. He was a poor relation of the parvenu family of Sir John Spencer, of Northamptonshire. Born in the early 1550's, he was about six when Elizabeth came to the throne, and died in his mid-forties four years before her. His life thus pretty well coincided with that glorious but difficult time.

It was a time much like ours in its rugged individualism, its sensational rise of the uncultivated vulgar to responsible riches. With a sense of her provincialism, her cultural inferiority, England looked sturdily and emulously across to proud France and prouder Italy, determined to "overgo" them in poetry and scholarship and power, which she eventually did and has. With a lift from some unknown hand, or hands, Spenser got the best of schooling at Merchant Taylors, went on to Cambridge, was there recognized for his talents by the discerning; became secretary to Dr. John Young, Bishop of Rochester, and so on and up to Court, then the only road to a career, where he became at once associated with the great but not good Earl of Leicester and with his more famous and more upright nephew, Sir Philip Sidney. This was doing pretty well for a citizen's son in his twenties. It was a high and dizzy atmosphere for the young cockney idealist. He went a little heady with his success and the hope of preferment, the attention of the great, the social ferment, the discovery by himself and certain of his friends that he was already an eminent poet, perhaps the very one who was to revive English poetry.

Then something happened, apparently some idealistic indiscretion which led him into dangerous satirical comment on affairs of the great, not for such as him to meddle with—the much discussed marriage of Elizabeth, or the calculating maneuvers of Burleigh, or the graft of the great clergy, or the sensual worldliness of the Court. All of these come in for open chastisement or veiled criticism in his *Shepherds' Calendar* and *Mother Hubbard's Tale*. He proved an uncomfortable inconvenience to the great, and was sent to Ireland as Lord Grey's secretary. There he lived the remaining twenty years of his life, essentially in exile. Twice he tried to establish himself again at Court, but in vain.

This cultivated pet of the Muses was suddenly plunged into the brutal frontier conditions of miserable, turbulent Ireland to make his way. It was as if one of our most admired literary prize men, launched like Fortune's favorite in the diplomatic service, were suddenly sent to keep order for the rest of his life in Mindanao. Or worse. But the experience was essential to the greatness of Spenser's poetry; it strengthened its fiber, and imparted to it fresh beauty. One who has looked upon the unearthly loveliness of Ireland, of which Spenser was fully aware, sees and feels it constantly reappearing in his song.

A sharp cleavage between good and bad, right and wrong, persists in Spenser. It may have derived from his experience both at a Renaissance court and in the shifting disorder of Ireland. Twice he has with intense feeling drawn the contrast between good and bad courtiers—the first time, during his first experience at Court, in his trenchant satire *Mother Hubbard's Tale*. There he found vulgar display of clothes and outfit, every mean, tricky little shift of getting on, servility, licentiousness, gluttony, drunkenness; you dare not trust anyone; everywhere graft and dirty deals in produce and real estate, especially in church property; everywhere restless change, everywhere scandal and lies; everywhere ignorant vulgarity that scorns learning and religion.

> Full little knowest thou that hast not tried,
> What hell it is, in suing long to bide:
> To lose good days, that might be better spent;
> To waste long nights in pensive discontent;
> To speed today, to be put back tomorrow;
> To feed on hope, to pine with fear and sorrow;
> To have thy prince's grace, yet want her peer's;
> To have thy asking, yet wait many years;
> To fret thy soul with crosses and with cares;
> To eat thy heart through comfortless despairs;
> To fawn, to crouch, to wait, to ride, to run,
> To spend, to give, to want, to be undone.
> Unhappy wight, born to disastrous end,
> That doth his life in so long tendance spend.

Happily he discovers a saving remnant, such as Sir Philip Sidney,

> the brave Courtier, in whose beauteous thought
> Regard of honour harbours more than ought.

Here one, there another of the better breed, unmoved by scandal and vice on every hand, walking upright with comely steadfast gait, accomplished in athletics, intelligently and actively interested in music, poetry, learning, in the manners and theory of chivalric Love, men who know the world, and employ all their talents and accomplishments in the service not of themselves but of their Queen and country.

Ten years later, when Spenser returned from Ireland for a year and more in and about Court, he observed and recorded in his *Colin Clouts Come Home Again* much the same state of things—the same vulgar ostentation and oafish incapability of finer things, the same cut-throat competition, the same slander, treachery, and betrayal, the same carnal and licentious cult of love. But this time he sets against it the glorious figure of Cynthia or Elizabeth, patroness of learning and song, who gathers about her honest, able, and energetic men. And then suddenly, the bitter satirist shows himself the true idealist that he is, by contrasting with the vulgar, sensual cult of love at Court the poet's noble conception of Love derived from Plato, as a divine, primal, essential, and metaphysical force, ordering the universe, reconciling hostile energies, inspiring the creative instinct to generate a higher and higher civilization.

> So love is lord of all the world by right,
> And rules the creatures by his pow'rful saw:
> All being made the vassals of his might,
> Through secret sense which thereto doth them draw.
> Thus ought all lovers of their lord to deem:
> And with chaste heart to honour him alway:
> But whoso else doth otherwise esteem,
> Are outlaws, and his lore do disobey.
> For their desire is base, and doth not merit
> The name of love, but of disloyal lust:
> Nor 'mongst true lovers they shall place inherit,
> But as exiles out of his court be thrust.

Now, making all allowance for literary and social conventionalities which entered into the framing of these criticisms of the Court—for poets had uttered them before, times out of mind—they exhibit the sharp dichotomy or division of Spenser's world which was the counterpart of a sharp antinomy in himself. For Spenser, the idealistic poet, all his life craved fame and hoped for worldly success. He would become a man of consequence and wealth in that Elizabethan world of bold enterprise, and quick profits. But he would not stoop to the current means of so becoming. They revolted him. Over against them arose within him his expanding vision of the true Realities, his conviction that Love, beginning however low down, is the only mounting Guide of Life, the only progressive Interpreter of Truth and Beauty, the only reliable Determinant of Action, being indeed an emanation of Very God Himself. In short Spenser is a confirmed Christian Platonist after Dante's kind, though born into a later time when agreed convictions had weakened.

But was there any basis in fact and experience for Spenser's idealism, such as Beatrice laid for Dante? In his early days in London a mysterious lady, masked as Rosalind, who could not or would not love him, bade fair to break his heart. He sings volubly, dolefully, but mysteriously about her, and her memory sweetly haunts him ten years after when, nearly forty, he returns from Ireland. Of course, the proud, cruel lady was a fashionable accessory, and every young man in high life felt it necessary to display at least a noticeable nick in his heart. But however conventionally Spenser may have entered into the affair with Rosalind, with his sonnets and his complaints *à la mode,* there are moments when his voice takes on the deeper resonance of sincerity. We have some reason to think that Spenser married during his first period at Court. If he did, she was not Rosalind. Then, when he was past forty, came the grand affair with Elizabeth Boyle. She was a capable and attractive woman by all we know, a kinswoman of the Earl of Cork; she married again soon after Spenser's death—in fact twice. But that is beside the mark. The point is that in those particular sonnets which all agree were addressed to Elizabeth Boyle, and supremely in his *Epithalamion,* the greatest wedding-song in the world, he sings with the same full-throated ease, the same happy assurance that we hear in the contemporary and mature *Hymn of Heavenly Love* and *Hymn of Heavenly Beauty*. Out of his earlier affairs of the heart, whatever they may have been, he has attained to a discovery of the metaphysical, spiritual, nay, religious potentialities of Love. And if the old worldly hankerings still bother him, he knows them for what they are, and is safely weary of them. Three years before he died, on his second return to Court, he composed what seems to have been his last verse, a lovely betrothal song for two young acquaintances. It begins:

> Calm was the day, and through the trembling air,
> Sweet breathing Zephyrus did softly play
> A gentle spirit, that lightly did delay
> Hot Titan's beams, which then did glister fair:
> When I whom sullen care,
> Through discontent of my long fruitless stay
> In princes' court, and expectation vain
> Of idle hopes, which still do fly away,
> Like empty shadows, did afflict my brain,
> Walk'd forth to ease my pain
> Along the shore of silver streaming *Thames*,
> Whose rooty banks, the which his river hems,
> Was painted all with variable flowers,
> And all the meads adorn'd with dainty gems,
> Fit to deck maidens' bow'rs,
> And crown their paramours,
> Against the bridal day, which is not long:
> Sweet Thames run softly, till I end my song.

So Spenser, like Dante, like many another idealist, found himself living in a carnal, self-seeking, ruthless, slanderous, mutable, crude, uncouth world. But there were two sides of it. He loved England, he saw a saving remnant in the capable men about him. And England became incarnate, romanticised, glorified, in the person of the Queen.

In 1596 he dedicated to her the six books of his *Faery Queen* in these terms:

> To the most high, mighty and magnificent Empress renowned for piety, virtue, and all gracious government, ELIZABETH, by the grace of God Queen of England, France and Ireland, and of Virginia, Defender of the Faith, etc., her most humble servant, Edmund Spenser, doth in all humility dedicate, present, and consecrate these his labours to live with the eternity of her fame.

It is easy but ill-considered to say that he merely flattered her. It is easy, at this distance, to find—or invent—her picturesque faults, as clever people do in print, and on the screen. But the great woman, in the charm of her actual presence, cast a spell on Spenser as upon other men of genius whom she drew about her. She released their creative power. She was a Queen, not a King, and all that was left of medieval chivalry idealized her into an incarnation of England, a militant heroine inseparable in imagination from the brave, young new nation who was saving herself from those proud old foes, the Papacy, Spain, and France, that had for centuries held her in contempt. Spenser belonged to the party that hated and feared these foes with an active hatred, the party of Leicester, Raleigh, and the Sidneys. With some risk of being misunderstood I may call it the Puritan party, for it stood for purification of the Church from the corruption still persisting from Catholic days. The most enlightened of these men, of whom Spenser was one, envisioned a better, cleaner, more stable England, which by the talents of the best Englishmen could hold her glorious own amid the threats of her corrupt and effete enemies.

What, then, could an idealistic young poet do about it? He was a misfit in that rough world, and for any trouble he took about it found himself pitched out into a far rougher one.

He believed in the power of Love to civilize, enlighten, and propel men's souls. Love, then, should civilize, enlighten, and propel his England into something better and so save it. And it should reach the hearts of Englishmen through beauty, through the beauty of poetry. He could, and he would, sing and charm them into greatness of living. We have already heard him uttering his faith in poetry as a subtle and enchanting influence to virtue. It was a creed he shared with Sidney and others of his time. I say "of his time"; but as a veteran teacher I have seen enough in my own time to convince me that he was right.

All which will, I trust, better enable us to see what the *Faery Queen* is about. The great poem was begun during Spenser's youthful experience at Court, before 1580. In 1590 he brought back from Ireland the first three books for publication. To these he appended a letter addressed to Sir Walter Raleigh, his sponsor, setting forth the whole intention of his poem. He said: "The general end therefore of all the book is to fashion a gentleman or noble person in virtuous and gentle discipline." To effect this he transports us to an imaginary land and an imaginary court of an imaginary Queen. In it he revives the romances of medieval chivalry, already a bit out of fashion, with all their moral black and white, their enchantments, magic, heroism, and turpitude. But the parallel with the world of Elizabeth, and indeed with the world at any time, is constantly in the mind of a reader who falls under the poem's spell.

In 1596 three more books appeared, and after Spenser's death two detached cantos on Mutability. The poem was to have gone to four times its present length, had the original plan been fulfilled. But it will serve as it is. Three years after its second installment, during which he seems to have written nothing, perhaps from worry about Irish unrest, perhaps because the vein would not flow, the storm of the Tyrone rebellion swept Spenser's Kilcolman Castle to ruin. Leaving wife and children in Cork, he rushed to London to give his agonized report of the disaster. In a few days, at less than fifty, he was dead, probably from exhaustion which made him easy prey to anything.

The *Faery Queen* is an allegory. So is the *Divine Comedy.* So is the *Pilgrim's Progress.* So are most of Shelley's longer poems. So are chapters in the Book of Ezekiel. So is the Book of Revelation. So are the most exalted passages in Plato. Yet today men balk at allegory and even resent it.

But in the face of such grand instances it is well for us to reason together for a moment on the matter of allegory.

The old critics speak of allegory as a veil. And such it is; at its lowest terms it may be a decent covering for something disagreeable or dangerous or satirical. But it is also a veil which reveals. Your experience, let us suppose, has generated in you conceptions so high, so incommunicable, so desperately important to the world that you must find some concrete medium of transmitting them to your own generation and generations to come. This, I take it, was the situation in which Dante and Bunyan and Plato and St. John and the Hebrew prophet and the poet Spenser found themselves. We saw Dante in despair of telling us what he saw, and Spenser has like moments; as no doubt had all the rest.

So the veil reveals as well as conceals, and may do both at the same time. For it makes the reader actively curious as to the poet's meaning, sets him guessing, rouses him out of a merely receptive state, takes him into a kind of active cooperation with the poet, indeed makes him poet too for the time; and the insight which he thus gains, he has earned; it is his own by right of effort, and he values it far more than if he had received it passively as mere information. Such is the ancient, practical, and, so far as I can see, the valid theory of allegory.

Why, then, has so glorious an implement lost its use? Well, it has not—at least not as an instrument of satire. Our cartoons are brief fragments of allegory, sometimes our films;

and anyone who remembers the devastating power of Rae-makers's cartoons in the other war may realize the terrible power latent in this medium, if it should come into the way of a great poet's imagination.

Why, then, do men now resent allegory, moral or anagogical? If it is obvious, they resent the implied insult to their intelligence, or to their behavior, which probably is no better than it ought to be, anyway. But if they are enthusiastically interested in moral ideas and growth, if they believe ardently in the invisible and burn to explore it, if they would know the Truth and be free, then allegory, any allegory which embodies the help of a seer to this effect, becomes endlessly fruitful to them. Or to put it in terms more commonplace, if the reader is interested in the poet's ideas, he will be interested in his allegory.

The great allegorists whom we have named had in their time a high advantage over any poet who might dare to attempt spiritual allegory today. They had behind them a more or less systematized community of belief and symbol, traditional for centuries, settled into definite form, inherited and accepted by their own generation. Such was the system of Thomas Aquinas to Dante, such the accumulation of Greek mythology and theology to Plato, such Calvin's system to Bunyan. Thus each of these had a frame, a code of symbol, a system of living and verified ideas which made their allegory interesting and important and intelligible; and according as the element of universal truth passed from these great men into their allegories, such allegories, even though partly apprehended, are interesting now and for ever.

Spenser's case is somewhat modified. The rich medieval symbols used by Dante were still in the world, and he used them. But the medieval frame was weakening, especially in England, and the Calvinistic frame, which was eventually to take possession of so many English minds, had not yet sufficiently settled upon them, or upon him. Still to his lively Christian faith he added his natural affinity for the ideas of Plato, and to these his heartfelt acceptance of Aristotle's ethical theory of the mean and extremes of the passions. These theories he had tested in his contention with evil in the world about him, as well as in himself. And out of this amalgamation of ideas, transmuting it with his glorious and supreme gift of song, he made the *Faery Queen.*

The medieval critics loved to distinguish four meanings in allegory—the literal, the natural, the moral, and the anagogical. In practice they did not always stick to the theory. In Spenser's allegory there are often two ulterior meanings, the historical and the moral.

He sometimes veils historical events or goings-on which his contemporaries had no difficulty in recognizing, but which have given modern scholars much to busy themselves about. Such events range from the struggle with the Papacy and the issue between Mary Queen of Scots and Elizabeth down to obscure little personal affairs at Court no longer recognizable, and not worth remembering. No doubt some of these passages amounted to mere compliment or pleasantry, though they were of large "news value" at the time; and we can imagine ladies and gentlemen in corners speculating deliciously on this or that allusion in this sensational new poem, to a marriage, an exploit, a little *coup,* a success, or a scandal at Court. Such devices, faded as they now are, no doubt had enormous value of allurement, and set people reading and talking about the poem until, without their being fully aware, it began to do some of them the good they needed, and "their trained wills entice."

But the moral allegory is more important. Sometimes it is too obvious to suit our more sophisticated taste, as in the allegory of the three ladies who represent respectively Aristotle's Mean and his two extremes of Excess and Deficiency of the Passions, the lovely Medina, the immodest Perissa, the grudging Elissa, and who entertain accordingly three appropriate knights. One must allow, as the critics do not, for a little diverting play on Spenser's part with such an idea. The critics find no humor in Spenser, probably from their own lack of it at the right time. As for the very ingenious and intentionally amusing allegory of the human body in Canto 9 of Book II, it disgusts them because they fail to catch the little gleam of delight in Spenser's eye, that trace of a smile, as he plays with his own ingenuities.

Let us pause for a moment over Spenser's scheme of his great work. It was no doubt a matter of much thought, of much shopping for right material in old legend, of much adjusting of part to part, and certainly of the exquisite joyful pain of composition.

The *Faery Queen,* as we have it, consists of six books and a fragment of another. The scheme is that of the Faery Queen's Court, that is, Elizabeth's, and each book was to represent the quest of a single knight, who more or less represents one of her great courtiers. But he also represents a single dominant virtue; some of these virtues, Temperance and Justice, are suggested by Aristotle. The six are Holiness for Book I; Temperance or Continence for Book II; Chastity for Book III; Friendship for Book IV; Justice for Book V; and Courtesy for Book VI. But the scheme is not so rigorous as it sounds. The allegory, whether historical or moral, comes and goes, flushes faint or florid in the surface of the narrative, or dies out altogether, leaving the story as a mere *exemplum* or illustration, but always in itself a good stirring or moving tale.

People who make jokes about the length of the *Faery Queen,* and the endurance required to finish it, either have not read it, or have tried to read it through from end to end, as you would read one of the contemporary dreadnoughts of fiction; which in point of fact are much longer, and once read are done with. Not so the *Faery Queen,* which you take up and lay down, ever catching its glowing pictures and gorgeous pageantry in new unearthly lights, and hearing new and compelling strains in its transcendent music. I cannot hope in a brief moment to demonstrate the slow, deep, and subtle effects of the *Faery Queen* that come from long habitual reading of the poem. At first of course the mind is captured by more sensuous qualities—the pageantry, pictures, color, music, motion. This is as it should be, as Spenser intended. But other and subtler effects set in unawares and through these very agencies, until we find ourselves caught in willing chains and sweet captivity of the imagination, and we know it is good for us—for our hearts, our minds, and our wills. We wander with Spenser through a succession of old stories, old lore, old symbolism transmuted by his touch, mellowed by his magic. We find it no dream world, no "escape" world so much sought by the moderns, but a rejuvenating world, conceived to inspire and correct our praxis in the real world, in very deed "to fashion a gentleman or noble person in virtuous and gentle discipline," which translated, means "to train and mold an exceptional person into a man of good life and manners." And this is not to be accomplished by reiteration of precept, but by weaving mysterious influences about his mind, starting ideas, sensitizing his feelings, enlarging his capacities, awakening and directing his imagination, opening his eyes to the invisible realities, and so through the influences of personified Justice, Self-Control, Decency, Courtesy, but above all of Love, moving him to express himself not only with his lips, but in his life, to the enlightenment of the world around him. This is poetry plus. This is Spenser's intention. He saw around him a greedy, sensual, treacherous, self-destructive world. He saw that it could be saved only by a few of the best. It was for these, in his hope of a greater England, nay, a better world, that he devised his *Faery Queen*.

For brief instance let us take the First Book. It chooses the old theme, the voyage of life, the *psychomachia,* as the learned call it, the battle of the soul. It is the theme of the *Divine Com-*

edy, of the morality plays, of the ancient story of Faust, of the Book of Job, of the *Pilgrim's Progress,* of Tannhäuser. The Red Cross Knight, St. George, Young England, a thoroughbred, grows up on a farm, and generously offers himself to the cause of delivering the parents of the pure and lovely Una from a besieging Dragon. With her, he easily overcomes an untidy monster, called Error or bad education, but is immediately after as easily fooled by false appearance and human duplicity into a hasty false inference, which slanders Una and causes him to desert her. He is then easily picked up by the false but speciously beautiful Duessa, who carries him to the Court of Pride, where he is preoccupied with the Seven Deadly Sins on parade, and with the gorgeous and idle crowd. A pagan knight, Sans Joy, picks a quarrel with him, but as Red Cross is getting the best of the fight, Sans Joy vanishes, and Red Cross, baffled and distrustful of the whole business, quietly withdraws from the Palace. He next encounters the wind-bag giant, Orgoglio (Conceit), and is overcome and thrown into a dungeon, while the false and treacherous Duessa gives herself to Orgoglio. But Una, the lady, has not been idle. Through various adventures she learns of Red Cross's fall, and goes with the valiant Prince Arthur to deliver him. Poor Red Cross is a sorry sight when he emerges from Orgoglio's dungeon. Una, sweet, generous, loving thing that she is, excuses all his misbehavior as the fault of the stars. But escape from moral failure for Red Cross, or for any man of character and a devoted heart, is not so easy. He encounters old man Despair who drives him to suicide, or would have done, had not Una interfered in the very moment of his act, reminding him of his appointed task undertaken for her sake.

Una then takes him to the House of the aged Lady Celia, or Holiness, where she dwells with her three daughters, Faith, Hope, and Charity. It is a charming domestic scene transcribed no doubt from some hospitable English country-house where

Spenser had been entertained. At Una's request Hope clears Red Cross's mind, and he is overcome with shame at the full realization of his infidelity to Una, just as Dante had been overcome in the Earthly Paradise. But he is saved from utter despair by Hope, and undergoes a terrible ordeal of penitence and purgation. Then Charity instructs him in the supreme doctrine of Love, and he visits the hospital of the seven beadsmen or the seven good works, founded by Charity—another exquisite transcription from the English scene. Thence he proceeds to the chapel of an old hermit, Contemplation, on a hill, who conducts him to the highest mount whence he gains a beatific vision of the Heavenly Jerusalem. Ravished with the sight he cries

> O let me not (quoth he) then turn again
>> Back to the world, whose joys so fruitless are;
>> But let me here for aye in peace remain,
>> Or straightway on that last long voyage fare,
>> That nothing may my present hope impair.
>> That may not be (said he) nor mayst thou yit
>> Forego that royal maid's bequeathed care,
> Who did her cause into thy hand commit,
> Till from her cursed foe thou have her freely quit.

> O holy Sire (quoth he) how shall I 'quite
>> The many favours I with thee have found,
>> That hast my name and nation read aright,
>> And taught the way that does to heaven bound?
>> This said, adown he looked to the ground,
>> To have return'd, but dazed were his eyne,
>> Through passing brightness, which did quite confound
> His feeble sense, and too exceeding shine.
> So dark are earthly things compar'd to things divine.

> At last whenas himself he 'gan to find,
>> To Una back he cast him to retire;
>> Who him awaited still with pensive mind.

> Great thanks and goodly meed to that good sire,
> He thence departing gave for his pain's hire.
> So came to Una, who him joy'd to see,
> And after little rest, 'gan him desire,
> Of her adventure mindful for to be.
> So leave they take of Celia, and her daughters three.

And thus, a new man, or rather his real self come true, Red Cross overcomes the terrible dragon after three days of fighting and frees Una's aged parents. The last canto is a charming finale, with the pageantry of the betrothal, the last desperate but vain attempt of Duessa, and the departure of Red Cross to report to the Faery Queen, whence he will in due time return to his wedding.

It is obvious that here we have the allegory of a typical young Englishman of the better sort—or a young American?—reared close to the soil, safely overcoming the bewilderment of ideas to which he is exposed in his education, but not proof against false conceit, self-reproach, failure, and despair, the very dangers and ills which beset young folk. From these it is only true Love which can save him and raise him through penitence, discipline, and contemplation, to a true sense of the Invisible, the Beatific Vision of the Divine Presence.

Thus Spenser, like Dante, reveals himself a mystic, one who believes that this vision is possible, that it comes only by suffering and purgation, and that it fortifies and reinforces a man for reliable answer to all the demands that life can make upon him.

Such is the First Book. The schemes of the other books vary. They are not always so methodical as this. But they are invariably ingenious and full of suggestion. The grand lonely figure of Britomart, the woman warrior, who moves with such power and mystery through three of the books—she is a living, human embodiment of the compound idea of England and Elizabeth of which I spoke earlier, reticent, passionately tender at times, unselfish, invariably reliable, outraged and stung to action by evil; one who puts to redeeming shame for their weak susceptibilities all the decent men with whom she comes in contact. She is one of the classic creations of literature, like Odysseus, Iphigenia, Helen, Faust, Cordelia.

It is an interesting and significant and sobering spectacle, that of a great poet, plunged into a barbaric, disordered world, torn and tossed and whirled about by it, convinced more and more deeply of its shifting mutability, its hopeless degeneration, yet at the same time laying faster hold upon the supreme reality of Love as the only creative, sustaining, and redeeming Power. In his *Complaints,* in his prose tract, *A View of the Present State of Ireland,* in many an incidental passage, Spenser gives free utterance to his despairs. Such release no doubt did him good.

But in the *Four Hymns* we may discern a Platonic Christian mysticism through the course of its development closely similar to that of Dante. It begins in actual romantic, even sensual experience, as shown in the first two hymns, which seem to have been first written in his earlier years. They are the *Hymn of Love,* addressed to Eros or Cupid, as an elemental god, and the *Hymn of Beauty,* addressed to Aphrodite, or Venus, and embodying the Renaissance Platonic philosophy of Beauty so cherished by Italian poets and others. But in the companion and supplementary hymns, the third, *Of Heavenly Love,* and the fourth, *Of Heavenly Beauty,* his voice expands to the fuller and deeper quality characteristic of his latest poetry, and his melody, always free, moves with the even energy of a deep-flowing river. Yet the variety of intonation, of instrumentation and orchestration, is exquisite.

Historically these four hymns, particularly the two Christian hymns, crown a long and ancient tradition, a tradition of two thousand years. From Plato and his pagan successors, through St. Paul and the early Fathers, through the later medieval mystics, especially in Italy and Spain; through a large accumulation of English literature, both Catholic and Protestant, continues this tradition of an ascent of the soul toward the Beatific Vision of God, or indeed of final identification with Him. Men and women experienced it, studied it, methodized it, wrote of it, sang of it, that others might also experience it as they had done. And by degrees they distinguished two avenues or routes of such ascent, the Theocentric and the Christocentric. Both involve first of all discipline such as qualified the Red Cross Knight for his ascent to the vision of the New Jerusalem—the discipline of penitence, good works, prayer, and contemplation.

But the Theocentric route of ascent proceeds by contemplation of the works of God, ascending from the study of Nature from lower to higher forms, at length to the stars in their spheres and orders, to the empyrean, the nine orders of angels, the Attributes of God, and thus to the Divine Presence. At once you will recognize Dante's course of ascent.

The Christocentric route of ascent proceeds by a contemplation of our Lord—the mystery of His humble birth, His life on earth in all its details, His Passion and Death, His Resurrection, His Ascension, His Glory, His Justice, but above all His Love—until at last we see Him face to face even while in the body. Again we shall recognize the Christocentric element in Dante's vision, especially at its close.

Now of the two crowning hymns of Spenser, the third, *Of Heavenly Love,* and the fourth, *Of Heavenly Beauty,* the third is Christocentric, the fourth, Theocentric.*

No exposition or comment can do justice to the third hymn. It demands a sympathetic reader with organ voice. Indeed, if you should adopt Spenser as your poet, be sure to read this hymn aloud at least every Christmas, and as much oftener as

* I am grateful to my friend, the Reverend Joseph B. Collins, and his recent book on Elizabethan mysticism, for this illuminating interpretation.

you can. I shall never forget a student of mine, not a brilliant man, who on an assignment had just read this hymn and read it aloud to himself. When he came in next morning, he seemed a little embarrassed and uneasy. Finally he blurted out: "That third hymn. I am not what you call a religious man. I don't understand those things. But it had me converted. I don't mean the argument. The music. It was the music. Things that sound that way *must* be true." Perhaps no criticism can surpass this.

The hymn, of 286 lines, falls into an invocation and three parts. It is thus exactly symmetrical with the other three. The invocation prays to be lifted up above the old and earthly loves that we may behold things invisible to mortal sight. In the first part Spenser reviews in terms of Plato's *Timaeus* and *Symposium* how, before all time, God created the Son through love, how the Holy Spirit emerged through them, how the Angels came into being, how a portion of them fell through Pride, and were cast into Hell, how Man was created from clay in God's image at length to take their places, how he too fell, and God through Love came to redeem him. Such is the first part.

The second is an impassioned apostrophe to the immeasurable Love which has given us everything, and asks no return but that we love Him and love our brethren for His sake, as He loved both them and us.

The third part exhorts us to meditate and review His life and sacrifice for us, until we are caught up to gaze upon His Light, which blinds all fleshly sight:

> Then rouse thyself, O Earth, out of thy soil,
> In which thou wallowest like to filthy swine,
> And dost thy mind in dirty pleasures moil,
> Unmindful of that dearest Lord of thine;
> Lift up to him thy heavy clouded eyne,
> That thou his sovereign bounty mayst behold,
> And read through love his mercies manifold.

Begin from first, where he encradled was
In simple cratch, wrapt in a wad of hay,
Between the toilful ox and humble ass,
And in what rags, and in how base array,
The glory of our heavenly riches lay,
When him the silly shepherds came to see,
Whom greatest princes sought on lowest knee.

From thence read on the story of his life,
His humble carriage, his unfaulty ways,
His cancred foes, his fights, his toil, his strife,
His pains, his poverty, his sharp assays
Through which he pass'd his miserable days,
Offending none, and doing good to all,
Yet being malic'd both of great and small.

And look at last, how of most wretched wights
He taken was, betray'd, and false accused;
How with most scornful taunts, and fell despites,
He was revil'd, disgrac'd, and foul abused,
How scourg'd, how crown'd, how buffeted, how bruised;
And lastly, how 'twixt robbers crucified,
With bitter wounds through hands, through feet, and side.

Then let thy flinty heart, that feels no pain,
Empierced be with pitiful remorse,
And let thy bowels bleed in every vein,
At sight of his most sacred heavenly corse,
So torn and mangled with malicious force,
And let thy soul, whose sins his sorrows wrought,
Melt into tears, and groan in grieved thought.

With sense whereof whilst so thy softened spirit
Is inly touch'd, and humbled with meek zeal,
Through meditation of his endless merit,
Lift up thy mind to th'author of thy weal,
And to his sovereign mercy do appeal,
Learn him to love, that loved thee so dear,
And in thy breast his blessed image bear.

With all thy heart, with all thy soul and mind,
Thou must him love, and his behests embrace;
All other loves, with which the world doth blind
Weak fancies, and stir up affection base,
Thou must renounce, and utterly displace,
And give thyself unto him full and free,
That full and freely gave himself to thee.

Then shalt thou feel thy spirit so possess'd,
And ravish'd with devouring great desire
Of his dear self, that shall thy feeble breast
Inflame with love, and set thee all on fire
With burning zeal, through every part entire,
That in no earthly thing thou shalt delight,
But in his sweet and amiable sight.

Thenceforth all world's desire will in thee die,
And all earth's glory, on which men do gaze,
Seem dirt and dross in thy pure sighted eye,
Compar'd to that celestial beauty's blaze,
Whose glorious beams all fleshly sense doth daze
With admiration of their passing light,
Blinding the eyes and lumining the spright.

Then shall thy ravish'd soul inspired be
With heavenly thoughts, far above human skill,
And thy bright radiant eyes shall plainly see
Th'idee of his pure glory present still
Before thy face, that all thy spirits shall fill
With sweet enragement of celestial love,
Kindled through sight of those fair things above.

Such is this mystical Christocentric song of Spenser. I cannot say whether he himself ever experienced the full ecstasy
of the mystic vision or identification. I do not know. He was in
part a man of the world, a bad world too, and had within him
instincts which enabled him to understand the attraction of
that world. But he also understood the redeeming power of

Love, love which first stirred on the lower levels of his youthful soul. Yet in time it interpreted to him the possibilities of the mystic ecstasy, and he realized at least, as again and again he says or implies, that the only deliverance from the world's deceptive evil and treacherous attraction is through Love as an elemental and divine agency, lifting us towards a comprehension of the Invisible.

If, then, Spenser is the man and poet for you, and you are the man for him, what may you expect from such a lifelong intimacy? Here I may speak from experience.

I would think first of all of the mere delight and rest to one's mind which radiate from the infinitely varied pictures in Spenser's gallery, from the pageantry and sound. "The ways," he says,

> In this delightful land of Faery
> Are so exceeding spacious and wide,
> And sprinkled with such sweet variety,
> Of all that pleasant is to ear or eye,
> That I nigh ravish'd with rare thoughts' delight,
> My tedious travail do forget thereby.

And his intimate friends will know exactly what he means.

Then it is amazing how much one learns through long association with this man; I mean particularly the encyclopedic knowledge useful to the understanding of the intellectual and spiritual history of the world. Like Dante or Milton, he is a fair substitute, to an unfortunately increasing number, for the study of the Latin and Greek classics. He abounds in ideas, not always accepted by him, but useful to him as a poet, because as they glitter and tumble about in his imagination they generate the music which is his poetry. This is not to accuse him of insincerity because it is easy to distinguish between the ideas he plays with and those he proclaims.

Then, there is the subtle but powerful effect of his music on both the mind and the speech of those who listen to him. For there is no adequate reading of Spenser, if of any poet, except with the voice. I do not mean that if you read him you will begin to write like him. But no other poet can do more than Spenser, if as much, to attune the cadences of your speech, to sensitize your ear to what is good, what ugly in sound, to generate in your public utterance that persuasive and fluent power of music in your speech, of which we have seen such an eloquent instance in Spenser's case.

But his effect is also intellectual and spiritual. He is not a mere phenomenalist, nor a mere magician with sight and sound. He insisted upon synthesis, difficult as it was in his confused and intoxicating time, and he insinuatingly compels synthesis in those who would be really intimate with him. He made up his mind. You must make up yours. It is a condition of getting on with him. You need not agree with him in all particulars. But if you go along with him at all you cannot escape his grand Platonic Christian conclusion. Whatever compromise you are tempted to make with the world—and I fear this is a besetting temptation of preachers as well as of teachers—and whatever adjustment to the ways and needs of the world is necessary, you have in your confidence this man who was of the world yet in his soul exalted safely above it.

And he is a man of insinuating charm, at least to those who can come close to him—more so than any of the other three we have chosen to consider. He is the most intimate of the four, the most responsive, the most accessible, the subtlest in exercising those rejuvenating influences which are transmitted by friendship with a great poet.

MILTON

As we travel along the literary highroad which leads from Spenser's day to Milton's, we pass through two generations. Somewhere along the way, about the end of the great Queen's reign and of her glorious century, the complexion of things has changed, and we emerge to realize that we are in a different cultural climate—a climate more like our own. The light is brighter, but only to reveal the world in its more literal reality. That other light which illuminated the transcendent reality of things, the light proceeding from the blending of Christian Platonism and medieval chivalry, which it often both veiled and at the same time magnified by allegory—that light has faded and disappeared. The very air we breathe now seems to contain more oxygen; it is more dense; yet it is harsher and somehow it elevates the spirits less than that which we left behind.

It may be that the climate of that other century—the century of Spenser and Elizabeth and Shakespeare—is the climate which best suits your spiritual health. In that case you may return and live there with that society which you find more congenial and excellent. But it may be that this new climate is your climate. If so, you will find the people here just as great and sustaining and fit for long acquaintance as those you left behind.

What accounts for this difference? Many things. If one tried to reduce it to fewest words, he might say: "The spirit of Lord Bacon has been released in the world." That man who, after the old encyclopedic habit, calmly took all knowledge for his province was an exponent of the new erudition, of the questioning of old authority, the reexamination and sifting of opinions and premises hitherto accepted from the Ancients, especially from Aristotle, the new appeal to fact particularly in the physical world. In short, Science and the scientific method of inquiry for truth had entered upon the long campaign which has in these some three or four hundred years since come to dominate men's minds and thinking. This may be—indeed is—for better and for worse. It has highly intensified our scrutiny of certain vast areas of life, particularly the physical area, and incalculably improved the physical conditions of living, so that a poor man today lives more safely and comfortably than any prince of the old time. But the old powers of imagination and spiritual preoccupation had already, even in Milton's time, begun to show signs of slackening, and these signs were discernible, at least to such prophetic vision as his. In the prelude to the Ninth Book of *Paradise Lost* Milton utters his misgivings lest "an age too late" should defeat his song and prevent his rising to the demands of his high theme. Did he mean "an age too late" for the grand poetic imagination to seize upon and body forth in compelling song the truth of the Invisible?

I fancy Milton's contemporaries looked back upon the Elizabethans much as we look back upon the Victorians, now two generations gone. Some despised the rosy Elizabethan illusions, Elizabethan chivalry, Elizabethan doctrines of Platonic love, and scorned the amateurish romanticism of their Elizabethan grandfathers. Others mourned wistfully for the mellow glamor of the good old Elizabethan days, and tried to continue it by imitation. Milton, whose earlier poetry still retains much Elizabethan charm, and who all his life studied the art and fed upon the ideas of Spenser, caught and comprised much of Spenser's very quality in his deep and sustained diapason.

But Milton is nearer than our other exemplars to the profession of the Christian ministry in America—particularly of the Presbyterian ministry. This may be an advantage and a recommendation. It may not. It may be most expedient for you to cultivate a poet as far removed from your immediate profession as possible. You must decide. At all events Milton was a Puritan born, and bred at the Puritan University, Cambridge, one of those Puritans out of whom came the civilization of our New England, and by that token essentially the prevailing civilization of our whole American Commonwealth. He was deeply in love with liberty, and all his life was bent on discerning its true nature and how it is to be won and preserved among men. Indeed he threw his whole heart and the energy of his genius into the struggle for English liberty that it might be propagated to the ends of the earth. A part of that struggle was his war against bishops for the cause of presbytery. And when he found that the victorious Presbyterians were inclined in their turn to use the old tyrannical methods—that, as he so wittily said, "new presbyter was but old priest writ large"—he moved with the Independents. Eventually he departed from orthodox Calvinism in an Arian direction, perhaps in the end to become a sect of one by himself. It was a time when sects were multiplying at an almost geometrical rate. This did not disturb Milton. In his immortal half-poetic prose essay on the liberty of the press, his *Areopagitica,* he pleads passionately for no restraint of honest opinion. Let all honest ideas and views circulate freely. Have you no faith in Divine Truth and its power to survive? Mistaken sects and opinions will die naturally when exposed to the open sunshine. Truth alone will thrive and prevail therein. Hence thought and honest utterance of opinion must be free. We have naught to fear and everything to gain by such freedom and liberty. This at least is the first premise in Milton's theory of liberty, and must be a comfort to us nowadays.

We cannot remind ourselves too often that interest in politics, art, education, ecclesiastical questions, even as late as Milton's day, still involved an interest in theology. These fields of inquiry were not posted preserves as nowadays, but parts of one big common, and presented various aspects of the one concern. And the theological aspect of truth occupied Milton more and more; with theology of course went the study of the Hebrew language, literature, and civilization. This explains why Milton has peculiarly attracted the Protestant mind, even the orthodox mind, which has been surprisingly slow to suspect him of his heresies. For perhaps thirty years prior to 1658, when his continuous work on *Paradise Lost* had begun, he was compiling his *De Doctrina Christiana,* a system of theology constructed on the proof-text plan, based in some measure on Ames and Wolleb. Perhaps he made it to settle in his own mind what he believed, perhaps to construct a definite mold or frame of thought for his great epic. Or both.

But this is only to indicate one of the innumerable dimensions of the man's mind. Besides theology and ecclesiastical polity, and liberty of the press, such subjects as divorce and what we call "social" problems, education, politics, history both of England and Muscovy, grammar, lexicography, with incidental and learned allusion to much else, such as music and mathematics, suggest his range. His treatise on education contains within its brief compass more good sense on these matters than I could cite elsewhere in many times the space. His *Areopagitica* will never fail to thrill and exalt the human heart with its reasoned and inspired apotheosis of true liberty. All these excursions in many directions he made as he says, "in the cool element of prose." He escapes classification by any category of human endeavor—any, that is, but as "poet" in the largest sense of the term, the maker, the architectonic artist, the super-mind, the genius with encyclopedic range and a talent for song such as God has vouchsafed to but few since the world began.

I wish we had a *Milton Dictionary,* like the *Dante Dictionary* by Toynbee. We shall have it some day, of course. Meanwhile the superb Index of the Columbia *Milton* will serve. Whatever its other uses to readers of Milton such a dictionary would exhibit the wide circumference, the extended horizon circle, the encyclopedia, of Milton's mind. For his generation is about the last to entertain the encyclopedic conception of learning, the aspiration of one man to embrace the full round of all knowledge. It was a conception doomed soon to burst under pressure of the weight and bulk of knowledge heaping higher and higher by human industry and discovery. But the encyclopedic conception of knowledge was of enormous importance to the universality of a poet, and now that it has become no longer possible, poetry has suffered, and shrunk, like all other occupations, into specialized and limited functions. We have nature poets, love poets, romantic poets, religious poets, Hoosier poets, the voice of California or of Vermont. Nobody would think of calling Milton just a nature poet, a religious poet, a romantic poet, a classic poet, for he is all these and more.

There is, however, one limitation of Milton's range. His disgust with the history of the later medieval Church, with its cruel intolerance and fear of liberty, and with the corrupting survival of such abuses in the English Church, his anti-Catholicism, gradually made him proof against the influence of ancient ecclesiastical traditions which beautifully expressed themselves in symbol, rite, and the arts—traditions, as we have seen, of immeasurable value to the art of Dante and Spenser.

But this is partly compensated by Milton's profound erudition in Greek culture. From the time when he was a small boy he breathed the spirit of Latin and Greek literature and history with every breath. To him it was the breath of life. For to Milton the classics represented not mere erudition, but the essence of poetry. He wrote Latin verse as if it were English, and used it to express some of his deepest grief and his most impassioned desires. He finds himself in no situation, visited by no experience, entertaining no enterprise which does not suggest to him spontaneously a parallel in ancient history or poetic myth. All of which lends not only deep and delicate resonance to his song, but capaciousness to his ideas and grandeur to his narrative. It may be just this very grandeur and spaciousness of Milton's mind which frightens away readers nowadays. He demands, or seems to demand, too much effort from them. We would take our literary pleasure more passively than he allows us to. But I maintain that it is good for any of us who is emotionally and mentally alive, particularly for a spiritual ministrant to his kind, to dwell within the immediate range of a mind like Milton's, to submit to its expanding power, to transcend with him the petty particularities that constantly shorten our focus, to see little things as little by seeing great things as great, thus to grow into a power of control which will economize, order, and turn to account all our efforts.

Milton, then, is, with all his achievements, the poet or maker. This he proves not alone by his multifarious acquisitions of mind, but by his control thereof, by the simplicity of form to which he reduces them. What in its broad array, such as a *Milton Dictionary* would demonstrate, seems hopeless complexity, he refines and subjects to the simplest form. His heaped accumulation of materials never gets the best of him. In the end or final effect every detail is functioning in its place.

One instance will do as well as another. In his tragedy, *Samson Agonistes,* he began with the grand but rather crude story of a primitive hero as told in the Book of Judges. To this he added the best learned comment he could get. To this he brought years of reading, or rather appropriating, the Greek tragedies of Aeschylus, Sophocles, and Euripides. To this he brought his own suffering of blindness, of disillusionment, of depression, of hopeful triumph over them through his Christian Stoicism. Samson he shows at the focal point in his captivity just on the eve of his death and triumph, whence all his previous life, his failures and successes and divine mission, are viewed in perspective or retrospective, or are drawn into concentrated power, somewhat as in a dramatic monologue. The whole at last assumes the form of that simplest Greek tragedy, the *Prometheus Bound* of Aeschylus, and the figure of Samson stands forth in the most obvious and unadorned and apparently unstudied dignity. But it is a different Samson from the Hebrew Samson in Judges, refined as it is by the thousand resources upon which Milton drew, yet always under his shaping control as a poet. Such architectonic power, such structural control, is of course characteristic of the great poet at any time. We have observed it in Dante. But in Milton it is more extraordinary for the variety and extent of the material which he has gathered and which he subjects to artistic regimentation.

And this brings us to what is, I think, the master key to an intelligent and useful appreciation of Milton. It was somehow a mysteriously great feat to draw his vast encyclopedia into the simple and clear focus of his various poems. Furthermore it was a feat which he first performed on smaller scale in his earliest great work, his *Hymn on the Nativity,* written of a Christmas morning when he had just turned twenty-one. Nor was the secret of it in the study of the great classical models, nor in the mere force of his own intellect. In the prelude of the Hymn just mentioned, in a cadence as lovely as any he ever, with Spenser's help, invented, he sings:

> See how from far upon the Eastern road
> The Star-led Wizards haste with odours sweet;
> O run, prevent them with thy humble ode,
> And lay it lowly at His blessed feet;
> Have thou the honour first, thy Lord to greet,
> And join thy voice unto the Angel Choir,
> From out his secret Altar touch'd with hallow'd fire.

He would outstrip any who come bearing the secular wisdom and power of all the earth in their hands, bringing a richer store than they, yet with simplest faith and humblest surrender of heart and voice, devoting all to "the Heav'n-born-child, All meanly wrapt in the rude manger." This simple faith of Milton transcended, controlled, and ordered, I believe, all his learning, even his elaborate theological refinements. It was a synthesis which kept ever in control all the complex elements with which he worked.

Would it not be good for us, in the stress of our ministrations to the spiritual needs of men, if we could from time to time quietly lose ourselves in the vast spaces and infinite multiplicity of the cathedral at Chartres or Canterbury, where every one of the multitudinous details is subject to the grand simple ground-plan of the Cross? Such, I conceive, may be the effect of retiring often into companionship with Milton.

But with Milton this molding of infinite riches into simple form was not so simple or so easy as here it may sound.

His life long he was prone to the Renaissance lust for Fame —"That last infirmity of noble mind." It might be a noble infirmity, but to him it *was* an infirmity and a besetting one. He was dazzled by the glories of preeminent learning. The reader, once aware of it, can discern his sense of this weakness in his writings of every period.

Moral issues were ever uppermost in Milton's mind, as in what first-rate poet are they not? In Milton they constantly relate themselves in some way or other to this besetting infirmity, this agonizing temptation, this lust of erudition, this exulting pride in learning for its own sake. Shakespeare, with exquisite wit and discernment, speaks of "the scholar's melancholy, which is emulation." To Milton it was not exactly a melancholy, but a temptation to misappropriate his great powers, the center of conflict always renewing itself.

In *Paradise Lost* his portrait of the fiend Belial, limned with intense but restrained feeling, reveals this fallen archangel as the universalized learned dilettante, erudite, sophisticated, vain and ostentatious of his culture, diffusing scholarly contempt, revelling in his erudition for its own sake, yet believing in nothing but his own elegant ease.

> He seem'd
> For dignity compos'd and high exploit:
> But all was false and hollow; though his tongue
> Dropp'd manna, and could make the worse appear
> The better reason, to perplex and dash
> Maturest counsels: for his thoughts were low;
> To vice industrious, but to nobler deeds
> Timorous and slothful: yet he pleas'd the ear,
> And with persuasive accent thus began.

Such Milton had no doubt seen among the learned of his day, and such, but for the grace of God, he himself might become.

Even more eloquent is the instance in *Paradise Regained,* wherein Christ recovers Paradise for fallen Mankind, not as we should expect, by His Passion, but by His Temptation in the wilderness.

Milton in general follows the Gospel narrative of this event, but departs so far from it as to make the crowning temptation a vision from the mountain, of the glory of ancient Rome and Greece, and a glorification of humanistic culture. Says Satan:

> Be famous then
> By wisdom; as thy Empire must extend,
> So let extend thy mind o'er all the world,
> In knowledge, all things in it comprehend.

And Christ replies:

> Many books
> Wise men have said are wearisome; who reads
> Incessantly, and to his reading brings not
> A spirit and judgment equal or superior,
>
> (And what he brings, what needs he elsewhere seek?)
> Uncertain and unsettl'd still remains,
> Deep vers'd in books and shallow in himself,

Crude or intoxicate, collecting toys
And trifles for choice matters, worth a sponge;
As children gathering pebbles on the shore.

Is it possible that the aged Milton here renounces, as it were, his lifetime of learning, and retracts his lifelong and passionate devotion to it? I think not. Rather, like a prophet he proclaims to all teachers and scholars—yes, and I fear to some preachers —the essential impairment and devaluation of all their work unless their minds are centrally made up, unless all their lucubration, their attempts to train or edify others, nay, all things they say or do, are polarized, or rather, animated, by a central conviction, a synthesis. It is essentially the solution, already cited, at which St. Paul and St. Augustine arrived.

The career of John Milton, rehearsed in many a text-book, is pretty familiar. I would, however, review it to illustrate certain values which it lent to his poetry. Born of prosperous cockney middle-class family, bred classically at St. Paul's and Cambridge, with light upon him from his father's eyes—and his mother's too—possibly a bit spoiled, he spent after college six comfortable years at home in a sweet little hamlet up the Thames, reading voraciously, hobnobbing at will with the Sciences, the Muses, and congenial friends. Occasionally he tried his maturing voice in song—in the *Nativity Hymn* while still at Cambridge, in those flawless idylls, *L'Allegro* and *Il Penseroso,* in *Comus.* Amid flights reminiscent of Spenser one catches premonitory measures in the fuller Miltonic diapason, which was to become his natural quality of utterance in the greater poems. When he was nearly thirty came *Lycidas;* then more than a year of tremendous expansion in Italy, where all those golden years of reading came true. Then follow the twenty years, roughly between thirty and fifty, when he was sterile in song, prolific in pamphlets, spending his seraphic energies in teaching not very receptive youngsters, in the diversified discussion we have already noticed, in defending his country before all Europe for repudiating and finally beheading its king, in writing diplomatic Latin documents for the government, in devising a new constitution for England. When it began to be clear to him that the great experiment of the Commonwealth might fail, he turned again to poetry and produced the three great works of his later age *Paradise Lost, Paradise Regained,* and *Samson Agonistes.* And then in 1674, at sixty-six, he died.

Certain critical moments or periods of this life are more significant than its events. We must not forget that this man even in his youth became aware, not from being told but from inner promptings, that God had given him the seer's eye and the poet's voice, that he was a genius of high order, set apart for some great achievement. The conviction was not a comfortable one. At the University it bred an arrogance which made him unpopular. At twenty-three he had to defend this conviction from the reproach of his friends. Such a gift demands not only development but creative exercise. Hence arise unhappy conflicts for any able young man. For a genius of Milton's order they are excruciating. He discovered early that the Church toward whose ministry he had been looking might inhibit his powers. He felt stirring within him some great work which the world would not willingly let die. At about thirty the many sheltered years of happy preparation suddenly turned bitter and sour, perhaps from delay. Fears haunted him lest he should be cut off in his youth, or dawdle away his life, indifferent even to Fame. Such bitterness and fears and self-reproach mingle with his young indignation at the state of the world, to temper and reinforce the quality of *Lycidas,* and give it the deep and sustained undertone to which he had not hitherto attained.

Then come the twenty songless years when poetry was suspended for more prosaic tasks, and when he was at last overtaken by slowly progressive blindness. What now had become of that one talent "which was death to hide?" Milton has been much blamed for this defection from poetry; but it is my conviction that he could not help it.

Great creative artist that he was, he well knew the mysterious behavior of what we call inspiration—how intermittent, unpredictable, uninducible, uncontrollable is the power of song. In later life at least it came upon him only from spring to autumn, and was usually strongest while the nightingale was in song. At that it visited him only, or chiefly, in the hours just before dawn, or even in his sleep. The poets, when they talk about this mystery, as they rarely do, agree as to these suspensions of spontaneous creative power, inspiration, visitation of the Muses, call it what they will. And I cannot think otherwise than that in Milton's case, during those two precious decades, his Heavenly Muse stayed away. What, then, if she should never come again, if his great task were to be unfulfilled—if blindness had intervened to forestall her irrevocably? Meanwhile his preparations for the grand poem had been going on, the more prosaic shop-work—such as reading, meditating his subject, sketching and revising his plans.

Two external crises, his ill-advised and impulsive marriage at thirty-three and his blindness at forty-four, seem to have shaken his very foundations. Then, after the old power did return undefeated, and at fifty composition of *Paradise Lost* had begun, he saw his beloved England, just as she seemed about to enter upon an Earthly Paradise of civil liberty, and claim that Paradise for all the world, relinquish her high endeavor, turn back, and abandon herself again to the old fleshpots and idolatries. Is it strange that one who had weathered such misgivings and disillusionment should lean with all his weight on Christian Stoicism and proclaim in his poetry the glories of "Patience and heroic Martyrdom"? Nor was he embittered, as hasty observers infer. By testimony of his biographers and other documentary evidence, "Though fallen on evil days, On evil days though fallen," he continued cheerful, tranquil, affectionate to the end. Poet or no poet, such a man it is good to know.

I cannot better economize time and space, than to quote in full the memorable prelude to the Third Book of *Paradise Lost,* which embodies in one way or other most of the observations already made, and much more: his belief in his divine inspiration, his passionate commitment to his sacred theme, his poetic sensibility to sights and sounds in Nature, his old habitual sense of parallel between his case and cases in the ancient world, his reconciliation to his blindness, his affectionate nature, his inclination at the close to a Theocentric mysticism, which manifested itself sporadically through his life.

> Hail, Holy Light, offspring of Heav'n first-born,
> Or of th' Eternal Coeternal beam
> May I express thee unblam'd? since God is light,
> And never but in unapproached light
> Dwelt from Eternity, dwelt then in thee,
> Bright effluence of bright essence increate.
> Or hear'st thou rather pure ethereal stream,
> Whose fountain who shall tell? before the sun,
> Before the Heavens thou wert, and at the voice
> Of God, as with a mantle didst invest
> The rising world of waters dark and deep,
> Won from the void and formless infinite.
> Thee I revisit now with bolder wing,
> Escap'd the *Stygian* pool, though long detain'd
> In that obscure sojourn, while in my flight
> Through utter and through middle darkness borne
> With other notes than to th' *Orphean* lyre
> I sung of *Chaos* and *Eternal Night,*
> Taught by the Heav'nly Muse to venture down
> The dark descent, and up to reascend,
> Though hard and rare: thee I revisit safe,
> And feel thy sov'reign vital lamp; but thou

Revisit'st not these eyes, that roll in vain
To find thy piercing ray, and find no dawn;
So thick a drop serene hath quench'd their orbs,
Or dim suffusion veil'd. Yet not the more
Cease I to wander where the Muses haunt
Clear spring, or shady grove, or sunny hill,
Smit with the love of sacred song; but chief
Thee *Sion* and the flow'ry brooks beneath
That wash thy hallow'd feet, and warbling flow,
Nightly I visit: nor sometimes forget
Those other two equal'd with me in fate,
So were I equal'd with them in renown,
Blind *Thamyris* and blind *Maeonides*,
And *Tiresias* and *Phineus* prophets old.
Then feed on thoughts, that voluntary move
Harmonious numbers; as the wakeful bird
Sings darkling, and in shadiest covert hid
Tunes her nocturnal note. Thus with the year
Seasons return, but not to me returns
Day, or the sweet approach of ev'n or morn,
Or sight of vernal bloom, or summer's rose,
Or flocks, or herds, or human face divine;
But cloud instead, and ever-during dark
Surrounds me, from the cheerful ways of men
Cut off, and for the book of knowledge fair
Presented with a universal blank
Of nature's works to me expung'd and ras'd,
And wisdom at one entrance quite shut out.
So much the rather thou, Celestial Light,
Shine inward, and the mind through all her powers
Irradiate, there plant eyes, all mist from thence
Purge and disperse, that I may see and tell
Of things invisible to mortal sight.

At the beginning of the passage, you may observe, he identifies physical with spiritual light, according to his belief that the physical and the spiritual are not two, but one in various degrees of refinement. Such a view stands in contrast with that Neo-Platonic belief of Spenser and the Renaissance generally, a dualism in which matter was commonly conceived as a gross substance more or less resistant to permeation and impression by the Divine Idea. To Milton matter itself is divine and capable of infinite refinement toward the Divine Essence itself, and physical light is essentially one with the light which proceeds from God Himself.

Such views as this may have led Milton to express the great theme of *Paradise Lost* in terms too physical for many listeners. He is more anthropomorphic than Dante or Spenser, say the critics, and they are quite right. This, I admit, may be a serious defect. With our habitual dualistic suspicion of matter, and our antinomy of physical and spiritual, we either object to, or even laugh at, certain passages in *Paradise Lost*—as when Adam and Eve entertain the angel Raphael at dinner—"no fear lest dinner cool"—or when the hosts of Heaven are dismayed by the artillery barrage of the Fallen Angels. I do not defend these passages—they do not bulk large in Milton. I only, for my part, set them down to curious amusement and do not read them any oftener than I have to. If in this scientific, economic age of mass brutality I could still see matter dignified as Milton saw it, I might understand this element of his work better. Meanwhile we have the close of the *Divine Comedy*.

If I found a young man who preferred the minor poems of Milton to his longer ones—the *Nativity Hymn*, the *Lines at a Solemn Music*, the idylls, *L'Allegro, Il Penseroso*, the *Comus*, the *Lycidas*—I would give him his head, and his heart too. For these contain in them the spring of Milton's later golden autumn. I would say, get them by heart. Their very music, in which the subtle virtues of Spenser's song live on, must purify and sweeten your own utterance. Then, their beautiful structural order, their exquisite, painstaking finish, to which Milton's experience in the classics was essential, their wealth of rare antique material made richer by Milton's touch, their

keen and healthy sense of the mysteries which surround us—
the mysteries of Nature, of the night and the sky and the sea,
of death and the life to come and the spiritual ascent, the poet's
delicate responsiveness to sights and sounds and other sensible
objects, their generous, sanguine, and youthful enthusiasms
and views, as yet undimmed and unsoiled by the obstacles and
dust which impede us in the midway of life: all these indicate
unfailing resources of delight and effective culture with which
the minor poems abound.

As for the great poems, *Paradise Lost* and *Paradise Regained*, they await rediscovery in our time. They are well
known, but not read; esteemed, but not appreciated. You may
have sampled them under dreary auspices of the schoolroom.
But who attempts to awaken their organ music now, to lay
them beside human life as we know it, to observe how vividly
and effectively they reflect it, and how authentic, bold, and
illuminating is their thrust into the mysteries of the ways of
God to men? They offer the enterprise of a lifetime.

In the greatest piece of literary criticism, and the best guide
for the teaching of literature ever written, Aristotle devised an
order of procedure for comprehending a piece of literature
which no teacher of literature can do without. It amounts in
effect to a consideration of five aspects of a poem: the sensuous
effects upon eye and ear; the plot or structure; the use of argument; the characters; and the diction and language.

I would therefore suggest to one who inclines toward
Milton, first to wander irresponsibly about in the vastness of
Paradise Lost and give himself up to the variety of things
strange and beautiful to see, to the grand music which rises and
falls and reverberates through those infinite spaces of the poem
from end to end. Let him not attempt at first to explain or
measure or locate anything, but simply luxuriate in the wealth
of the poem's sensuous beauty, taking care to read it aloud as

well as he can, and to imagine how he would make those deep, long-drawn cadences sound if he could.

I would then suggest, but not prescribe, a careful reading of the little arguments which introduce each book. For *Paradise Lost* is a supreme instance of Milton's power of reducing infinite matter to simple form. And its simple plan is this:

> Satan, an angel of highest rank in Heaven, grows envious and angry when the Son of God is exalted above him. He conspires against God with one third of the angels, but is defeated by the Son of God and driven headlong with his followers down into Hell. To repair this loss God creates Man with Woman, and places them in a garden of his new Universe in a state of free innocence. But Satan escapes from Hell, tempts Man through Woman, until they both violate God's Law. They are condemned to death through all generations, and can find redemption from their punishment only through a great sacrifice.

And to continue the story into the epilogue, *Paradise Regained,*

> Satan is driven by his own iniquity to tempt the Redeemer hopelessly and in vain, whereby Man is redeemed, and Satan is self-destined to be for ever bored by hopeless and unprofitable struggle to corrupt mankind.

Nothing could be simpler. Yet nothing could give a man— even a superman of Milton's stature—more room to say what he knew about matters of deepest import. It involves all space, all time, all mankind. You may recognize in this plot the simple outline sketched by Spenser in his *Hymn of Heavenly Love.* Some will even say that Milton took the plan from Spenser. Certainly it was the result as he says of "long choosing and beginning late." For many years ere he began regular composition, he had meditated a long list of other themes, sketched scenario after scenario, chosen and abandoned a dramatic form, and manipulated his matter in various experimental molds.

In growing familiar with this great work it will of course be impossible, while you are considering one of these aspects specified by Aristotle, altogether to exclude the others; for character determines plot, and expresses itself in argument and language. Yet, as Aristotle avers, the story or plot is the most important consideration, since it is by what happens that the poem or drama performs its proper effect, and gives its proper pleasure.

The greatest plots of play or poem or novel are simple. This plot is simple. Keeping its simplicity throughout, Milton has interwoven with it the tradition of Lucifer's fall, so that it is a two-fold plot, the tragic course of Mankind sprung from the tragic course of Satan. But these two are intertwined into one mainly by the logical sequence of the one from the other, and by a common motive. Satan fell because he set his heart on more sway than properly belonged to him. Eve, and so Mankind, fell because she set her heart on more sway than properly belonged to her. This present wayward world is reeling toward its fall because men have set their hearts on more sway than properly belongs to them. Which shows how immediate and universal is Milton's motivation of the old story. He understood as well as Dante, or Chaucer, or Spenser, how profoundly Pride, or Superbia, or Selfishness, is the deadliest of the Seven Deadly Sins, and the begetter of all the others, be they six or a million.

Consistently with the events and motivation of the old plot, Milton has fashioned his characters—Satan, his henchmen, Adam, Eve, the Angels; and he has dignified the story by universalizing these characters and by clothing the whole plot in most elaborate explication of speech, character, action, simile, setting, and dramatization, which, elaborate as they are, never for a moment neglect or hide the simple theme beneath.

This internal relation of part with part, this right emphasis and just subordination, this articulation by countless filaments, is one of the most astonishing resources of this poem. Some of the filaments are obvious, some so delicate that the reader discovers them only after long association, though their function has not been idle.

In epic poems it is customary to distinguish between what is main narrative, and what is called episode. The games in Homer and Virgil are episodes. But in Milton the episodes, if episodes they be, are so articulated with the theme that one would not know well how to prove them episodes. Even Milton's similes wrought after the extended epic fashion have been shown to run parallel to the matter which they illustrate, not in one particular, but in many unspecified, but no less effective, details. Which will, I hope, suggest the illimitable opportunity in this poem for the study of that paramount virtue of great art—including the art of homiletics—architectonic structure.

This same architectonic virtue manifests itself peculiarly in Milton's skill in the art of argument, what Aristotle calls *Dianoia*. Schooled as he was in the orators of Greece and Rome, in all the devices of logic and rhetoric and oratory known to Aristotle and Cicero and Quintilian, and developed through nearly two thousand years of continuous study and practice, it is not strange that he made poetic use of this skill whenever right occasion offered. Not only did it enter subtly into the texture and articulation of his work, but is the very sinew of the speeches in *Comus, Paradise Lost, Paradise Regained,* and *Samson Agonistes.* Long and intelligent regard for these speeches must have its salutary effect upon one who has a case to present, upon his regard for the nature of his audience, upon the ordering of his argument, upon his use of devices and resources for making it convincing, upon his conception of structural form, thus economizing and rendering more effective the convictions and energies which should marshal all these devices and carry conviction into the souls of other men.

In representation of human nature or character, that ability by which most writers are judged nowadays, Shakespeare's reputation always stands first. But his task was quite different from Milton's. He presented men and women in their vast variety. But Milton was dealing in a peculiar sense with all time, all space, all mankind, and must not only generalize, but heighten his generalization with reinforcement of personality. In the case of Satan, for example, he had to create not simply a criminal, a bad man of one sort or another, Iago, Antonio, or the composite bad man, but one who embodied the transcendent power of begetting evil in others, whether by false reasoning, intrigue, infectious enthusiasms, or sheer force of an irresistible and fascinating personality. This Milton has done with his Satan, and it is perhaps his most difficult feat. At any rate nothing has been more misunderstood, or led to more perverse judgment of the poet. People glance at Satan in his first dazzling entry upon the scene, go their ways and say that Satan was Milton's hero in spite of himself. They think it a joke on Milton. If they would but follow Satan through to his last, dismal case, they might have clearer notions, not alone of Milton's Satan, but of the real nature of evil and damnation, its cause, prevention, and cure, than they could gain from Dante or any other poet. They would be contemplating a person and course of events into which have entered the best ethical wisdom of the ancients, Plato, Aristotle, and the Stoics, and united with it the best that Milton could learn from Christianity and Holy Writ, not to say from bad men he had known.

Satan first appears fascinating, great, but a bit artful, with his professions of generous sacrifice and his courage. The most dangerous men are so. He is the thriller, the spellbinder. Then, at the Council in Hell, he is exactly the arch political boss. Then he turns the sensational adventurer. Then we come upon him alone, torn with uncomfortable misgivings, with corollary passions of envy and spite, with ungovernable and unreasonable temper, privately stooping to any little trick or indignity or cover; then as the shameless and unsportsmanlike liar he circumvents Eve; then we behold his complete abandon to what he knows is mere unprofitable destruction, *Schadenfreude,* until he sinks to the lowest level of dreary boredom to which he has condemned himself, a routine of devastation in which even he does not believe and for which even he no longer has heart. It reads like the intimate biography of a dictator, highly magnified.

Along with Satan are his henchmen, archexamples of types we may easily recognize in conspicuous public figures—Moloch, the forthright believer in force only—Belial, the elegant but rotten dilettante—Mammon, the believer in material resources only, who talks business from the shoulder and talks it well—Beelzebub, the artful, discreet, political lieutenant, the right-hand man, reticent, watchful, opportune, who underreaches all the rest, and at last puts the Chief over without splitting the party. At the opposite pole from these worldly figures are the artless Adam and Eve. In Adam we meet again that charming, eager young enthusiast whom we first met in *Comus,* then all flushed with excitement of his reading in ancient poets and philosophers, sanguine in his conclusions—the young Milton himself in point of fact. But now, as Adam, he has become a bit less sanguine, a bit subdued.

Then follows the drama of the temptation and fall, and Adam and Eve in their unhappy disillusioned maturity, the Eternal Masculine and the Eternal Feminine, at first unreconciled, but at last brought in repentance and suffering to full understanding of each other. There is much in this for men to learn about women, and for women to learn about men. And lest there still be those who contend that Milton's judgment of such matters is untrustworthy because it is warped by Puritan prejudice and his domestic mistakes, let us observe that men of the world like Euripides and Chaucer and Spenser and

Dante and Shakespeare and Browning agree with him. For they all observe that the basis and germinal element of evil in men is their egoism, in women their love of social power and preeminence; that when man comes to tragic grief it is usually through some weakness or perversion of his sense by the influence of women; but, if regeneration comes to pass, it is woman who goes ahead of him and points the way, often the very woman through whom he fell; it is the woman who makes naught of sacrificing herself to save him. To such effect in whole or in part runs the story of Alcestis, of Dante and Beatrice, of Una and Red Cross, of Hamlet and Macbeth and Isabella and Cordelia, of Browning's Sebald and Ottima. To such effect is the drama in seven scenes which constitutes the keystone and crisis of *Paradise Lost,* and forms the Ninth and a part of the Tenth Book of the poem. They divide the action thus:

I. Adam and Eve experience their first little difference. Eve, a bit restive and bored, wishes to leave Adam for an hour or two—certainly a reasonable and wholly innocent desire in itself. But in the warmth of the debate that follows Eve clearly is fretting at restraint as restraint, and Adam, just like a man, tries to assert an authority of superior wisdom which in his heart of hearts he knows his wife, in her heart of hearts, does not respect as much as he thinks she ought. Its verisimilitude to thousands of private domestic scenes every man should, and every woman will, recognize. There is no sin—as yet. But it is the first omen of a change of moral and spiritual weather for the worse that must startle and concern us if we are to minister to the spiritual needs of men. These omens Milton handles with most delicate, illuminating, and convincing power.

II. Satan encounters Eve alone, and with consummate skill and tact tempts her to her fall—not by flattery of her beauty, but by flattering her claim to a larger sphere of action and influence. But I must say he does not flatter her intelligence, except to make her think she has more than she has.

III. Adam discovers Eve's plight, and instead of using his wits to see whether, and how, he can save the situation, in rather doting and quite mistaken devotion, which he voices in noble terms of course, he succumbs to share Eve's fall.

IV. They both suffer disillusionment and recognize their utter nakedness of soul as well as body.

V. They accuse and blame each other.

VI. God judges them.

VII. Adam, entirely preoccupied with his own case, abandons himself to a paroxysm of extravagant grief. Eve tries to comfort him, but he brutally flings her away. Whereupon, like the Greek Alcestis—or any devoted woman—she offers her body and soul in retribution for the sin of both, that the man may be saved by her death. Her action brings Adam to his right mind, and they humbly confess their fault.

Here the story ends—except for the sentence of expulsion from the garden, and the grand vision of the future redemption to reassure Adam—"in calm of mind all passion spent." The closing lines are as moving and simple as any that Milton ever wrote.

Throughout the whole telling of the story the listener finds Milton's mind ever and again reverting to the subject of true and false liberty. You can quite reasonably view *Paradise Lost* as a poem on this theme. His finding, which owes much to the Greeks, he puts into the mouth of the Archangel Michael, by way of summary near the end:

> Know withal,
> Since thy original lapse, true liberty
> Is lost, which always with right reason dwells
> Twinn'd, and from her hath no dividual being:
> Reason in man obscur'd, or not obey'd,
> Immediately inordinate desires

And upstart passions catch the government
From reason, and to servitude reduce
Man till then free. Therefore since he permits
Within himself unworthy powers to reign
Over free reason, God in judgment just
Subjects him from without to violent lords;
Who oft as undeservedly enthral
His outward freedom: Tyranny must be,
Though to the tyrant thereby no excuse.
Yet sometimes nations will decline so low
From virtue, which is reason, that no wrong,
But justice, and some fatal curse annex'd
Deprives them of their outward liberty,
Their inward lost.

Words equally relevant and dateless whether they comment on the story of Adam and Eve, on seventeenth century England, or on the present state of the world. "Milton, thou shouldst be living at this hour."

Well, he may be, at least as an intimate companion of the individual. Like the other great ones he requires long and responsive, faithful association.

May I repeat an earlier word of admonition? I find it a present habit of students—superinduced, I think, by a generation of teachers too far gone in bibliographomania—to scant their scrutiny of an author's works and run off in search of something *about* them. Beware the habit. Your legs will never get strong enough to carry you, if you never walk without a crutch. You may have all of Milton's poetry in one well printed volume for little more than a dollar. Let inclination and curiosity be your guides. Mark favorite passages. Get them by heart. You are embarked on a romantic voyage of discovery. Enjoy the music and the spectacle, and ponder the meaning. What you discover by yourself is worth over and over what any authority can tell you. And if you look long and singly and humanly enough at the poem itself, probably you can tell the authority something. If the allusions in so learned a poet as Milton should trouble your classroom conscience, lay it asleep by enjoying the iridescent luster which their romantic remoteness lends to the texture of the poetry.

> High on a throne of royal state which far
> Outshone the wealth of Ormus and of Ind,
> Or where the gorgeous East with richest hand
> Showers on her kings barbaric pearl and gold,
> Satan exalted sat, by merit rais'd
> To that bad eminence; and from despair
> Thus high uplifted beyond hope, aspires
> Beyond thus high, insatiate to pursue
> Vain war with Heaven, and by success untaught
> His proud imaginations thus displayed.

"The wealth of Ormus and of Ind" is not increased by learning just what and where Ormus was; perhaps it is diminished. Anyhow the information on such a point is not indispensable to the enjoyment of this noble passage.

Years of association with Milton may serve as a worthy substitute for the old training in Latin and Greek language and literature out of which this generation has unhappily been cheated. His language is a glorious hybrid of vigorous English and the language of Virgil and Ovid. To possess yourself of Milton's language is in a measure to possess yourself of those virtues of style and utterance which your predecessors used to derive from wise teaching of Latin and Greek. But style is far more than a matter of grammar, idiom, and words. The sustained cadence and measured movement of Milton's voice must exert a purifying effect upon the voice of one who habitually listens to him. You will pick up from him in the long run a rich store of literary currency which will enable you to travel anywhere in the realms of gold without discount of exchange. He is charged as is no other poet of whom I know with the energies of Greece and Rome. He is indeed a classic with all the knowledge, all the order and harmony, all the humanism, all the art, all the transcendent universality that make a classic.

"Cold climate or an age too late." The discrediting of the imagination as a means to truth, the disintegration of the old synthesis. Alas, our own climate is colder than his with our detached and neutral scientific habits, our inevitable specialization, our inevitable doubts and uncertainties. Our age is later and rings not with the trumpet tones of a single voice uttering the communal conviction of its time, but is filled with the din and confusion of many voices. How salutary, then, to draw close to one who incarnated essentially the dateless synthesis and conviction for his own time, and indeed, like these others, for all times, to the utmost power of his genius.

Milton does not invite the altogether genial intimacy of Spenser or Johnson. You may not in his company so often encounter those moments of detachment from the physical, of something approaching disembodiment, as with Dante. But I know him as an older friend and brother from whose presence I never depart without a sense of expansion, and enlargement, of clarification of mind and accession of power, together with an exaltation of spirit.

JOHNSON

SIR LESLIE STEPHEN, the ripe and expert biographer in late Victorian days, once remarked in a reminiscent moment: "I had the good fortune when a boy, to read what is to me, I must confess, the most purely delightful of all books—I mean Boswell's *Life of Johnson*. I read it from cover to cover, backward and forward, over and over, through and through, till I nearly knew it by heart." On his deathbed he was still reading it, and "told his nurse that his enjoyment of books had begun, and would end with Boswell's *Life of Johnson*."

This last stage of our journey, from Milton to Johnson, descends into the open. The life of Johnson stands almost exactly one hundred years after that of Milton. Our way thither leads down from the rarer and more solitary heights of Parnassus, the high lonely tower of the poet, to the populous and cited plain—in fact to eighteenth century London, that great Georgian city of good sense, good taste, and substantial comfort. And for many of us this may be a more congenial refuge and resort, especially for those who are intellectually more sociable, who learn by the more common yet slower means of observation rather than by the more direct, convincing means of imagination, men whose natural idiom of expression is pitched in the lower key of wit and sense and prose, rather than in the higher range of poetic inspiration.

This eighteenth century London, so multifarious yet so single an embodiment of its tranquil and sanguine time, was incarnate in Johnson as in no other man. He loved it and it responded to him.

"The happiness of London is not to be conceived but by those who have been in it."

"No man at all intellectual is willing to leave London. No, Sir, when a man is tired of London he is tired of life."

"I live in the world, and I take . . . the color of the world as it moves along."

But nowhere in London did this super-personality shine as at a good inn, like the Mitre or the Crown and Anchor. Said he: "A tavern chair is the throne of human felicity." Into this playful remark enters no thought of lower conviviality—Johnson was a total abstainer the greater part of his life—but rather the excitement of that most exciting and innocent game of conversation, and the temporary sense of warm security from the black fears and imaginings that tortured his soul in solitude. For this king of men, as someone called him in his day, clung desperately to his friends. "A man, Sir, should keep his friendship in constant repair."

If any man entertains the false notion of Johnson which Macaulay has propagated, of a clumsy, gluttonous, ravening, unclean, truculent Johnson, who tore his meat and drank his tea in oceans, wiped his greasy hands on a dog, roared with sesquipedalian bow-wow—that man's first and whole duty to Johnson, and to himself, is speedily and utterly to efface that caricature from his mind. For Johnson was, as he considered himself, a polite man, welcome, and indeed in demand, at the dinnertables of the best houses in London. And he has made for us one of the best definitions of a gentleman. "Perfect good breeding," said he, "consists in having no particular mark of any profession." Among many other instances I commend to you on this point that scene in Johnson's fifty-eighth year, so beautifully staged by Boswell, in the library at the Queen's house. Johnson had the privileges of the library, and at the King's wish, was one day presented to His Majesty. After some conversation the King paid Johnson a high compliment. Later, when Johnson was asked if he had replied, he said: "No, Sir. When the King had said it, it was to be so. It was not for me to bandy civilities with my Sovereign." And there is that charming counter-idyll of Johnson and the little thick short-legged boy in Mr. Strahan's courtyard, when he said: "Some people tell you that they let themselves down to the capacity of their hearers. I never do that. I speak uniformly, in as intelligible a manner as I can." Which glimpses suffice to prove that Johnson was polite not by code, but by heart.

We shall do better from the start to take our notion of Johnson not from secondary but from authentic sources: from Sir Joshua Reynolds's penetrating and sympathetic portraits, imbued with the greatness of both painter and sitter; and of course from Boswell, first and last. But not all the time. There are Johnson's own writings. It is true that he said: "No man but a blockhead ever wrote, except for money." He had no mystical notions of inspiration, at least in his own case. "A man may write at any time, if he will set himself doggedly to it." Yet he was a genius and his written word as well as his spoken is often vibrant with his greatness. He scorned imitation: "No man ever became great by imitation." His poems, *London,* and *The Vanity of Human Wishes*, imitated Pope and Juvenal, as Pope had imitated Horace. Yet he could never read his own lines in the *Vanity* about the ills of a scholar's life without tears. His essays in the *Rambler* are ostensibly after the pattern of the *Spectator,* and he afterwards found them "too wordy," yet their fiber is tougher, and their wit more muscular. For the two years while he was engaged in turning off these essays at the rate of two a week, and for most if not all of the decade between 1745 and 1755, between the age of about thirty-six and forty-six, his best energies were consumed in producing what is the keystone of all his work, the *Dictionary,* written, as he says, "with little assistance of the learned, and without any patronage of the great; not in the soft obscurities of retirement, or under the shelter of academic bowers, but amidst inconvenience and distraction, in sickness and in sorrow."

At fifty he had indeed already lived a full life. Born in the proud little cathedral city of Lichfield, the son of an intelligent bookseller, poor and strangely unwell, he left unfinished his course at Pembroke, Oxford. At twenty-five he loved and married a widow twice his age. He failed at teaching school— an omen perhaps of his superior abilities—and at twenty-seven plunged without resources into the precarious chances of a hack-writer in London. He knocked down one insulting literary slavedriver with a big folio. "Sir, he was impertinent to me, and I beat him." The humiliation of literature which he beheld on every side, but which he could not tolerate, engendered in him for nearly twenty years the god-like scorn which at last he poured out in the memorable letter to Lord Chesterfield on the completion of the *Dictionary,* which concludes:

> Seven years, my Lord, have now past, since I waited in your outward rooms, or was repulsed from your door. . . . Having carried on my work thus far with so little obligation to any favourer of learning, I shall not be disappointed though I should conclude it, if less be possible, with less; for I have been long wakened from that dream of hope, in which I once boasted myself with so much exultation, my Lord, your Lordship's most humble, most obedient servant,
>
> Sam: Johnson

"No man," said he, "who ever lived by literature, has lived more independently than I have done."

Four years later occurs the well-known episode in which he writes the whole of the romance, *Rasselas,* on the pursuit of happiness, in the evenings of one week, to pay the last debts of his beloved mother. A hundred miles away she was dying, he knew, and he had not seen her for years. Daily he dashed off a note to her; most of these arrived too late.

Dear Honoured Mother:

   Neither your condition nor your character make it fit for me
to say much. You have been the best mother, and I believe the
best woman in the world. I thank you for your indulgence to me,
and beg forgiveness of all that I have done ill, and all that I
have omitted to do well. God grant you his Holy Spirit, and receive you to everlasting happiness, for Jesus Christ's sake. Amen.
Lord Jesus receive your spirit. Amen.

   I am, dear, dear mother,

                    Your dutiful son, Sam: Johnson.
Jan. 20, 1759.

By fifty-three many of his early friends were gone, and the
First Act of his life was ended. But the curtain rose again on
groups of various new friends, such as Burney, Goldsmith, Mr.
and Mrs. Thrale, and Reynolds, who were gravitating into the
charmed circle, when, on a day in May, 1763, the hour struck
which has been, and ever will be, through the ages, so momen-
tous to all friends of Johnson. The year before, the King had
granted Johnson a pension which relieved him from drudgery
and made him free to impart his genius to the world in his own
peculiar way. Then on that May afternoon, in Davies's back-
parlor, James Boswell first met Samuel Johnson. Boswell was
twenty-two, Johnson fifty-three. Boswell, young Edinburgh
student of the law, was divinely appointed to be a hunter of
human big game. Voltaire, Rousseau, Paoli were among the
greater heads which he brought home. But with Johnson there
was a difference; it was a deep and strange attraction on both
sides, no doubt partly paternal-filial. With all his eccentricities
and vanities, Boswell had a deal of Scotch charm. His genius
was the genius of portraiture and biography. The two men had
in common the biographical instinct. Said Johnson: "The biographical part of literature is what I love most." Indeed his
Lives of the Poets are his greatest literary work. Written near
the end of his life, they garner the full harvest of his wit and
insight and sympathy. They are galvanic in their vigor, an

unfailing store of mental nourishment and energy. Here then, between these two biographical geniuses was engendered the greatest secular biography ever written, Boswell's *Life of Johnson.*

During the remaining twenty years of Johnson's life Boswell contrived nearly every spring to make his expedition from Edinburgh to London, to find himself "exalted" as he says, by the extraordinary vigor and vivacity of Johnson's conversation. Early in their friendship Boswell conceived the purpose of making his great biographical portrait. He was mindful of Johnson's remarks that "nobody can write the life of a man, but those who have eat and drunk and lived in social intercourse with him." It was not a mere matter of recording the conversation in shorthand and writing up his notes afterwards, though that in itself is difficult enough. If you do not think so, try it sometime. But Boswell had to know what was good and what was not, what would keep, and what would stale. For nothing is so volatile and perishable as anecdote. Many an anecdote, sweet though it be at the time of it, goes flat when it has been set down. "Wit is wit," said Johnson, "and if good, will appear so at all times." This wit Boswell knew when he saw it. So we who are, and ever shall be, committed to the friendship of these two men never tire of the wit and wisdom of Johnson, but find it both sweeter and more pungent every time we savor it, even unto a thousand times.

But Boswell's art included more than such discernment, rare as it is. Nothing picturesque or droll or touching or impressive escaped his questing artistic eye. He evidently, as Professor Donald Stauffer has shown us, had familiarized himself with all the versatile technique and varieties of biography which this biographical century had brought to the highest point. We find him steering and surreptitiously manipulating his great subject, Johnson, into all sorts of situations and settings and backgrounds and human associations, sacrificing his own dignity, intellectual or physical, to draw something from Johnson, resorting to any device that might produce something worth keeping. He was an artist, and the artist transcends petty and literal fact without sacrificing it. For Boswell constantly protests the trouble he took to find the truth and give accurate report, and the discovered facts bear him out. His is a trustworthy book, but it is also a masterpiece of art, and he who enters in takes possession of imperishable reality.

I will not delay to take Johnson's measurements by the criteria which we first laid down for our spiritual ally. He qualifies by them all as anyone may prove for himself—even by the gift of song. And though his knowledge was not encyclopedic according to the ideal no longer attainable by his time, yet his mind still had the encyclopedic concept and capacity. His genius goes forth in a kind of radiating potential which manifests itself in his inexhaustible humanity, in his capacity for friendship by no means limited to his own time and place, and in his strange power to fertilize the talents of other men.

When one considers the infinite detail which Boswell had to manipulate in the *Life,* one is the more astonished at the singleness with which he has kept to his theme. Through them all, through every temptation to be interesting on something else that comes up—and Boswell could be interesting on anything personal—Johnson is ever central and in focus. Johnson pervades the book. But around this fixed solar center are circling multitudinous figures whose orbits are in one way or other affected or controlled by this center of gravity. The cast of persons in this book is well-nigh innumerable; and if not impressive enough as it is, yet is lengthened in the many other *Lives* which Johnson unconsciously provoked. Almost any of his acquaintance who could get hold of pen, ink, and paper fell instinctively and naturally to biographing him. Something about the man seemed to breed biography.

Johnson, like Ulysses, was a part of all that he had met. I have a habit when I see a new book in any way concerned with the eighteenth century, of turning to the index, to the letter J. There almost invariably is Johnson's name for at least one entry. Which does not mean that he was a busybody, concerned with everybody and everything in his day, but that his humanity was such that nearly everybody, and everything, in his day, from cats to kings, was somehow concerned with him, enough at least to make him a general exponent of his time.

Johnson's human potential also manifested itself in the more amiable form of an infinite capacity for friendship. Friends he must have, and in numbers. They gravitated to him. Yet he never took them for granted; he made his own effort to keep his friendships in constant repair, and lamented that "the most fatal disease of friendship is gradual decay." He seems even to have been scouting for friends. "I look upon every day lost in which I do not make a new acquaintance." There was nothing sentimental about his friendships. Nor did he indulge in the common arts of cultivating them. In that fierce sport of conversation, when sense and truth were the stakes, he spared no one, and tossed and gored friend or foe alike. But if a friend took amiss anything he said and came off nursing a bruise, Johnson was the first to apply the soothing word and ask forgiveness. Said Burke of him: "It is well, if when a man comes to die, he has nothing heavier upon his conscience than having been a little rough in conversation."

The range of his acquaintance alone is imposing. It included lords and ladies, blue stockings, gentlemen, physicians, clergymen, soldiers, tea-table ladies, petty tradesmen, scholars, publishers, children, actors and actresses, a rich brewer, a brilliant Italian literary tramp, the charming but unprincipled Richard Savage. He loved his negro servant Francis Barber, and by that love immortalized him. He loved the kind and improvident Robert Levett, with whom he shared his roof and substance, and whom he has commemorated in his most moving poem. His oft-rehearsed charity, or benevolence as they then called it, seems always more than charity, glorified as it is with the warmth and glow of his inexhaustible love of friends. That motley household which he drew about him under the shelter of his pension was held together by the centripetal power of his affection. He wrote of them: "Williams hates everybody; Levett hates Desmoulins, and does not love Williams; Desmoulins hates them both; Poll loves none of them." And there is that saintly episode near the end of his life when he rescued a poor woman from the gutter and took her home on his back, there to nurse and bring her into a better way of life. Not through his telling was this known. His silence about it, its single luminous beauty apart from all his abundant life, make it matter more for hagiography than biography.

Soon after he met Boswell he said: "Sir, I love the acquaintance of young people; because, in the first place, I don't like to think myself growing old. In the next place, young acquaintances must last longest, if they do last; and then, Sir, young men have more virtue than old men: they have more generous sentiments in every respect." At sixty-eight he exclaimed: "I value myself upon this, that there is nothing of the old man in my conversation." As he could love, so could he hate, and he hated fools, unthinking sentimentalists, and knaves. Which very hatred is but one measure of the pure and compelling power and the discernment of his affection.

A greater dimension of Johnson appears in the strange survival long since of his power to make friends. It reaches beyond his London and his generation to other lands and to other times, even to our own. He died more than 156 years ago, but he is still making friends, friends with himself, friends with each other. Two strangers meet. One quotes Johnson, or echoes a Johnsonian phrase. Then they are off, recognized brothers in the Johnsonian Freemasonry, rehearsing in antiphon the sounding sense of Johnson back and forth, familiar as an old song, but ever new. And the acquaintance under the benediction of Johnson's memory—nay, through the very infection of his undying humanity—takes root, grows, and deepens into a close and lifelong friendship. This is not a wishful fancy of mine. It has happened.

But Johnson's humanity amounted to genius. At least it was commensurate with his genius.

Out at Streatham Park, some eight miles to the south of London, Henry Thrale, the rich brewer, kept his country house. It became a second home for Johnson and the proper setting in good Georgian taste for Johnson during the Second, and best, Act of his life—those twenty ripe and brilliant years which occupy most of Boswell's true story. Here Mrs. Thrale swathed him in comfort and good cheer, and warmed him to some of his best conversation; for she was charming, lively, and keen, if not always exact. And here her substantial husband, through a quiet and understanding friendship between these two robust men, lent Johnson that sort of fundamental substratum, that concrete reinforcement, which men whose traffic is in ideas find in men of success in practical affairs. Whatever these two, Henry and Hester Thrale, did for Johnson—and it was much —they are amply repaid by the immortality that his friendship has given them. On the walls of his library Mr. Thrale hung portraits of the great Johnsonian Circle painted for him by Sir Joshua. There they looked gravely down on their originals, Burke, Burney, Garrick, Goldsmith, Reynolds himself, Thrale, Johnson, and others, drawn together by mutual magnetism of mind and wit and gust for living.

There is something about this fact which is almost symbolic of Johnson's quality—the fine eighteenth century interior of the library, its good taste, good sense, and good cheer, the excellent collection of books about the walls, and above, the portraiture of the greatest talents of England in their time—

an actor, a poet, a musician, a painter, a statesman, but dominating them all, as in the flesh he often dominated the Circle gathered about this room, Johnson, whom all acknowledged with fearful and affectionate reverence as their center. For, as Professor Tinker has pointed out, Johnson served as a sort of dynamic genius to all this array of divergent talents. To them he imparted the intellectual energy and direction which fertilized their various talents into the works of art they produced, the architectonic ideas which gave them form, and made these works far greater than they could otherwise have been. Garrick's acting; Goldsmith's plays, verse, lives, novels, and essays; Reynolds's portraits; Boswell's masterpiece—none could have been what it was without Johnson. In a sense he created them. Yet he could have equalled none of them by himself. Strange that he who had so little sense of the actor's art, so little eye for painting or ear for music, and perhaps not full appreciation of the finest things in Goldsmith or the art of Boswell, should have been the unfailing source to which they all repaired for the essential energies of their arts. They testify to it. And where they do not testify to it, their art yields evidence enough to a true Johnsonian of the dynamic company they have kept. Boswell again and again testifies to the animating power of Johnson's talk and personality. "He roused every intellectual power in me to the highest pitch." Boswell found himself exalted by its full glow "as if brought into another state of being." Sir Joshua confesses that Johnson brushed the rubbish out of his mind, and recommended to young artists the tonic of such companionship. "Clear your mind of cant." Let this ringing phrase once wake the resonance of your ear, and its echo will never die.

The sociability of that genial century brought forth an increasing number of clubs; and you can find no better instance of Johnson's centripetal attraction than the famous Literary Club. It was first proposed by Sir Joshua Reynolds, quite possibly to provide conditions for the irradiation of Johnson's genius. The date was 1764, just at the beginning of the great period. At first it included the immediate circle of talents who through friendship were nearest to Johnson. But during the rest of his life it grew to a much larger membership and included great scholars, peers, churchmen, gentlemen, men of letters such as Gibbon and Sheridan, and statesmen such as Charles James Fox. Who can doubt that its center of gravity was Johnson himself?

If you should some day become a good Johnsonian, you may find yourself pondering more and more this undying radiation of personality and intelligence from Johnson, still as efficacious as ever. How many the creative artists since his time who have confessed, consciously or unconsciously, to his generating power in themselves—Thackeray, Carlyle, Macaulay, Stevenson, Lord Tweedsmuir, Browning—among them Scots a plenty! To anxious inquirers I have often recommended daily Boswell above all textbooks in composition I know as a means of attaining to clear and vigorous expression. This is not mere enthusiastic theory; I could cite cases in proof.

I have often wondered whether it was the same with all great personalities of history, or would have been if they had had their Boswells; whether a Boswell divinely adapted and appointed to every such personality could have transmitted that personality as James Boswell has done in this almost unique instance, so that it should continue to impart vigor and vision to men from generation to generation. Supposing Homer, or Euripides, or Virgil, or Dante, or Thomas More, or Coleridge, or Washington had been attended by a Boswell who fitted their respective cases—would these men now be living as Johnson lives among men? It is one of those questions for useful but inconclusive debate which will not answer itself, but will incidentally raise and answer a good many other important questions. The fact remains that Johnson at least vicariously imparted his genius to the talents of his own day, and continues to fertilize the talents of men who get to know him, now after more than a century and a half. It is a mystery which we may ponder with reverence, but cannot wholly explain.

So we roam with Johnson and Boswell through that mellow yet stimulating and always alluring eighteenth century world. Wherein lies its charm? Is it in the stately drawing-rooms, the genial inns, the grandeur of St. Paul's at Easter, or the dim religious light of St. Clement Dane's on Good Friday; in the dignified Common Room of Pembroke College, Oxford, the staid domesticity of proud old Lichfield, the swarming streets and courts of London, the primitive and dour feudalism of the Hebrides? The scene has something to do with it. Is it in the genial warmth and good fellowship and humanity which seems to follow Johnson about like a magnetic field? Said he: "I look upon myself as a good humoured fellow." Yet, as Boswell retorted: "You are good natured, but not good humoured: you are irascible. You have not patience with folly and absurdity." Or is it the shafts of his wit, often rising through a conversation to surmount the whole discussion with a flashing rejoinder, and flood the case in point with light; nay, far more than that, to transcend the particular case, and become universal and appropriate to a thousand other cases current and recurrent in our experience, to the end of time? In no one of these elements does the secret lie, of course, but in the sum and combination of them all, with others which each may discover for himself.

When you become a qualified Johnsonian you will find that Johnson's wit is constantly leaping into your memory and your speech, called forth by all sorts of human combinations and incidents.

Someone, let us say, gets into a dither at missing a train or forgetting an engagement. Says Johnson: "Consider, Sir, how insignificant this will appear a twelvemonth hence." Someone gives you a book, perhaps his own. Your conscience, oppressed with the duty of reading it, is soothed by Johnson: "People seldom read a book which is given to them." Someone undiscouraged by the failure of one venture in happiness has tried another. Says Johnson: "It is the triumph of hope over experience." You hesitate over some little expense for the family's comfort. You recall Johnson's remark: "No money is better spent than what is laid out for domestick satisfaction." You envy an admired virtuoso with forty talents, till you hear Johnson's resonant: "A man may be so much of everything, that he is nothing of anything." Or, to the well-bred indifferent: "I do not love a man who is zealous for nothing."

Boswell's *Johnson* is a rich composition of jewels, not in the rough, but cut and highly polished, with a thousand facets flashing a fadeless light in every direction.

"If he be an infidel, he is an infidel as a dog is an infidel; that is to say, he has never thought upon the subject."

"It matters not how a man dies, but how he lives."

"Hell is paved with good intentions."

"All censure of a man's self is oblique praise."

"Nonsense can be defended but by nonsense."

"Every human being whose mind is not debauched will be willing to give all that he has to get knowledge."

"No, Sir, a man always makes himself greater as he increases his knowledge."

"To have the management of the mind is a great art, and it may be attained in a considerable degree by experience and habitual exercise."

"Getting money is not all a man's business; to cultivate kindness is a valuable part of the business of life."

"The greatest part of our knowledge is implicit faith."

"Every man is a worse man in proportion as he is unfit for the married state."

Torn thus from all context these specimens may seem a bit wilted. But their context in Boswell is not the only one in which they live. Life offers new contexts every day in which they resume all the vigor and freshness they had when Boswell first gathered them.

At this point let us pause for some consideration of ways and means to cultivate the friendship of Johnson. Begin with Boswell. Own a complete edition of the *Life,* without notes. And in the *Life* we always include Boswell's account of the *Tour of the Hebrides.* Read it as the early Methodists read their Bible, opening it here and there, reading, as it were, from the inside out, marking good passages, and thus by degrees sidling into the book rather than attempting at the first to read it through consecutively. You will know when the time has come to read it through. Some day you will find that your curiosity is ready for the help of George Birkbeck Hill, who has edited both the *Life* and the *Hebrides,* with an abundant and lively accumulation of fact and anecdote gathered from the rich store of that anecdotal century. The store has been increased by the more recent lucubrations of Mr. L. F. Powell. Nor will you wish to confine yourself to Boswell and his editors. For Johnson's writings are but an extension of Boswell's gazing-glass. In them you find the same wit, the same trenchant criticism of life, the same imagery and vibrant resonance, the same central and polarizing convictions as in Boswell.

In his preface to his great edition, Dr. Hill ventures the likely opinion that, next to Shakespeare, Johnson is quoted and misquoted, the most frequently of all our writers. What is the secret of life in his utterance? What keeps it so living and so sweet? I have often asked myself.

I think the answer begins with the *Dictionary,* which I ventured to call the keystone of all Johnson's work. Like the *Faery Queen* this is a well-known but unconsulted book. Most people have heard its definitions of "oats" or "network," but that is about all. They naturally think of it as a literary freak. Without doubt it is an amusing book. Why not? Johnson was an amusing man, often intentionally so. His diverting definitions in the first editions of the *Dictionary* are deliberate of course:

> *Loquacity,* too much talk.
> *Poetess,* a she-poet.
> *Presbyterian,* an abettor of presbytery or calvinistical discipline.
> *Pie,* any crust baked with something in it.

Contrast the *Oxford Dictionary's* definition: "A dish composed of meat, fowl, fish, fruit, or vegetables, etc., enclosed in or covered with a layer of paste, and baked." More filling, but less flavor. And why should not a definition have flavor? Such as this:

> *Pedantry,* awkward ostentation of useless learning.

Could it be more compact, to the point, living and vibrant with wit? The mind tingles with delight at the very expertness of these definitions. Boswell is quite right: they "indicate a genius of the highest rank." And incidentally they leave no doubt that this great Leviathan of words was taking his sport therein when he defined "network," or "cough," or

> *Fit,* a paroxysm or exacerbation of any intermittent distemper.

Read page after page of Johnson's expert definitions if you wish to discover the secret of his wit, and incidentally if you wish to enjoy yourself. He did not spend that decade framing definitions day after day, putting the whole energy and discernment of his mighty mind into them, without a very definite effect upon his style of utterance. You may observe the change by comparing his writings before, during, and after the composing of the *Dictionary.* You may observe too that in most of his durable remarks, whether written or spoken, lurks the soul of a definition. It is true in nearly all the citations I have made. May I add a half dozen?

"Criticism is a study by which men grow important and formidable at a very small expense."

"To talk in public, to think in solitude, to read and to hear, to inquire and answer inquiries, is the business of a scholar."

"Never speak of a man in his own presence. It is always indelicate, and may be offensive."

"When I find a Scotchman to whom an Englishman is as a Scotchman, that Scotchman shall be as an Englishman to me."

"No, Sir, the Irish are a fair people—they never speak well of one another."

Boswell himself suggests, besides definition, another secret of Johnson's wit. "It teemed," he says, "with point and imagery." One must recall that the Circle in their day looked upon conversation as a competitive game, in which a just and expressive image scored high. The question arose of superiority between two minor poets. "Sir," said Johnson, "there is no settling the point of precedency between a louse and a flea." And again, of certain ignorant religious enthusiasts not retained at Oxford: "What have they to do at an University who are not willing to be taught, but will presume to teach? Where is religion to be learnt but at an University? Sir, they were examined and found to be mighty ignorant fellows." "But," objects Boswell, "I am told they were good beings." Johnson: "I believe they might be good beings; but they were not fit to be in the University of Oxford. A cow is a very good animal in the field; but we turn her out of a garden." Who will make an enlightened study of Johnson's imagery?

Definition and imagery, and what else? I alleged for Johnson a few minutes ago the gift of song. I had not in mind the verses he wrote, but the peculiar ring and music of his speech which has carried his words into the ears of thousands since his time, there to sing for a lifetime. This tune grows upon one the longer one lives with Johnson. Sometimes you attempt to quote one of his remarks from memory, and something about it sounds dull, leaden, counterfeit. What is wrong? You compare it with the original and find that by your careless alteration of one or two words, the vibration is relaxed, the living tune has gone out of it. This conclusion is, I believe, unexceptionable, and is constantly proved by less exact Johnsonians. "I pride myself on this, that old age is never apparent in my conversation." Compare this with the ringing original above.

Somebody was one day disparaging the custom of quotation from the classics, once a highly fashionable literary grace. Johnson defended it: "No, Sir, it is a good thing; there is community of mind in it. Classical quotation is the parole of literary men all over the world." There is just this "community of mind" about Johnson's utterance which has made it the parole of thousands of literary and non-literary men all over the English-speaking world. The very phrase "community of mind" is alive with the full life and resonance of that vigorous soul.

Such community of mind he derived in part perhaps from his love of multifarious human life. He appealed "from the rules of criticism to nature." All one's conjectures and beliefs must be tested in the laboratory of life itself. He admired a man with "a great deal of knowledge of the world, fresh from life, not strained through books." And as Boswell says, "he loved business, loved to have his wisdom actually operate on real life." We have already seen him merged with the life of London, high and low.

But multifarious as that life was, Johnson never lost his way. He had considered and felt it in all its variety from being penniless in the gutter to conversing with the King. But he viewed it all with his mind made up to the simplest yet most transcendent conclusion, a conclusion to which we have direct but awed access through the little book published the year after his death, from private documents which Johnson put into the hands of his friend and publisher William Strahan shortly before the end. It is entitled *Prayers and Meditations*. It contains about ninety prayers, the first on his twenty-ninth birthday, while he was still a hackwriter in London. The other prayers are dated usually on his birthday, at the New Year, Good Friday, Easter, on the anniversary of his wife's death. At the beginning of 1781, his seventy-second year, he prays:

> Almighty God, merciful Father, who hast granted me such continuance of life, that I now see the beginning of another year, look with mercy upon me; as Thou grantest increase of years, grant increase of grace. Let me live to repent what I have done amiss, and by thy help so to regulate my future life, that I may obtain mercy when I appear before Thee, through the merits of Jesus Christ. Enable me, O Lord, to do my duty with a quiet mind; and take not from me thy Holy Spirit, but protect and bless me, for the sake of Jesus Christ. Amen.

Here we are alone with that other Johnson, the solitary, deeply melancholy Johnson, who, as he said, was half mad all his life, at least not sober. It is the Johnson who scorned sentimentality, yet whose great heart was deeply responsive to inexplicable human misery, and who, though he stoically rebuked emotionalism in others and in himself, yet on occasion gave way to tears. It is the Johnson who luxuriated in the old romances of chivalry, who loved old castles, and was awed by vast Gothic interiors, who shuddered at every suggestion of death. It was the romantic Johnson—the Johnson divided in hopeless and mind-wrecking strife with the solid Johnson which all London knew, the sociable Johnson of good sense and wit and practical wisdom. How did he reconcile these two warring elements within him and keep his balance? How but by the simple faith which he had tested through life itself, and a hard and realistic life too, and by which he ordered all his observation and experience.

It is easy to make fun of Johnson, or at least to regard him only as a picturesque source of amusement. It is easy to take unreasonable offense at his forthrightness, his fixity of opinion, to misconstrue his intolerance, and to make no proper allowance for what he called the "anfractuosities" of his mind. It is easy to sentimentalize about him—a treatment which he would have resented most of all. Resist such false impressions till you know him. Then they will no longer trouble you. For you will find him a loyal and understanding and manly friend, one whose salutary words keep ringing in your ear, one whose fortitude and wisdom reinforce your own, one in whose heart and mind there was room for all sorts and conditions of men, one who through deeper trials and loneliness than most of us know kept a simple faith, without mystic transports, which transcended and controlled all his multifarious knowledge and experience, and helps to clear your vision of the mists and vapors that drift and eddy athwart it in days like these.

INDEX

Active and Contemplative Life, 10, 50
Adam, 94, 97, 100-2
Aeschylus, 12, 85-6
Agnel, 44
Alcestis, 12, 101-2
Allegory, 39, 43, 56, 64-70, 80
Allusions, 104
Ancients. *See* Classics
Anecdote, 111
Anfractuosities, 125
Antonio, in *The Tempest*, 99
Architectonics, 20, 83, 86, 98, 116
Architecture, 5, 19, 20, 54
Argument, 95, 97-8, 101. *See* Order of Thought
Ariosto, 54
Aristotle, 25, 49, 54, 67, 80, 95, 97-9
Arnold, Matthew, 23-4
Art, 19, 26, 32, 50, 54, 82, 98, 116
Augustine, 5, 16, 22, 89

Bacon, Francis, 9, 80
Beatific Vision, 51-2, 72-3, 75-8, 92-4
Beatrice, 17, 24, 35-6, 39, 42-5, 48-9, 61, 101
Beauty, Sense of, 18-21, 23
Beelzebub, 100
Belacqua, 41
Belial, 87-8, 100
Bernard, 51
Bible, 6-8, 39, 65, 70, 85-6, 88, 99
Bibliographomania, 29, 103
Biography, 100, 110-11, 117-18
Boccaccio, 5, 54
Boniface VIII, 47
Boswell, James, 110-12; *Life of Johnson*, 106, 108, 111, 116, 119-20; *Journal of a Tour to the Hebrides*, 120
Boyle, Elizabeth, 61
Britomart, 55, 72
Brooks, Phillips, 16
Browne, Thomas, 11

Browning, 18, 28, 30, 101, 117
Buchan, John, Lord Tweedsmuir, 117
Bunyan, John, 16, 65-6, 70
Burke, Edmund, 113, 115-16
Burleigh. *See* Cecil
Burney, Charles, 110, 115
Byron, 30, 40

Cacciaguida, 33-4, 36
Calvinism, 66, 82
Cambridge, 57, 72, 89
Cant, 116
Canterbury Cathedral, 87
Carlyle, 117
Casella, 32, 44
Catullus, 12
Cecil, William, Lord Burleigh, 58
Celia, 70-1
Character, 45, 95, 97, 99-100
Chartres Cathedral, 87
Chaucer, 12, 30, 55, 97, 100
Chivalry, 26, 32, 59, 63, 80-1, 124
Christocentric Ascent, 74-8
Ciacco, 41
Cicero, 22, 98
Cimabue, 32
Classic, 103-4
Classics, The, 5, 14, 18, 24, 28, 32, 41, 54-5, 66, 78, 80, 84, 88, 92, 98-9, 104-5, 123
Coleridge, 117
Collins, Joseph, 74n.
Columbia *Milton*, 83
Community of Mind, 66, 123
Contemplative. *See* Active.
Conversation, 53, 107, 113, 115, 118, 122
Cordelia, 73, 101
Cornell University, 27
Court, The, 58-60, 64, 67-8
Credo, 27, 51
Criticism, 3, 4, 67, 75, 95, 122, 123

[127]